COMPUTER DICTIONARY FOR EVERYONE

OTHER BOOKS BY
DONALD D. SPENCER

COMPUTER DICTIONARY FOR EVERYONE

Donald D. Spencer
Computer Science Consultant

CHARLES SCRIBNER'S SONS
New York

To Kitty and Maxie

5 7 9 11 13 15 17 19   F/P   20 18 16 14 12 10 8 6

Printed in the United States of America
Library of Congress Catalog Card Number 79-67070
ISBN 0-684-16946-0

PHOTO CREDITS

The photographs are reproduced through the courtesy of American
Airlines, p. 53; Burroughs Corporation, pp. 120, 129, 145; IBM
Corporation, pp. 51, 91, 123, 189; Lear Siegler, Inc., p. 33; Montgomery
Ward, p. 122; Pacific Medical Center, p. 153; Sanders Associates Inc., p.
148; and Varian Data Systems, pp. 124, 127.

PREFACE

In the past fifteen years, the computer has become as commonplace as the jet airplane. Schools, businesses, governments, colleges, newspapers, hospitals, industrial plants, and thousands of other organizations — all use computers to process vast amounts of data. The computer touches the lives of nearly everyone. Each of us, whether layman, student, or computer science professional, will have problems with computer terminology from time to time, and it is the purpose of this book to provide a ready means of solving these problems.

The **Computer Dictionary For Everyone** is intended for several kinds of reader. It is a basic reference book for all students of computer science/data processing in schools and colleges. It is hoped that the teachers and businessmen will find it a useful source book. Programmers, systems analysts, and other computer users will find it a handy reference book.

The keynote of this book is clarity — without sacrifice of authority and definitional precision. All definitions are simple, and stand as independent units of explanation. Many important terms, such as data, digital computer, error, file, Hollerith card, information processing, job, minicomputer, object program, software, and teleprocessing, are explained in nontechnical language, simply and tersely. In a few cases where a special terminology is required, the expressions used are carefully defined, and related terms or concepts are indicated by cross references.

The author of this book has been in the front lines of the computer revolution since the late 1950's. Computer models, programming languages, computer manufacturers, and programming techniques have come and gone since those days of "vacuum tube" computers and machine language programming. Today's computer-based systems and equipment are literally generations ahead and orders of magnitude more effective than their early predecessors. Because of the author's close involvement with computer science education and the design and use of computer-based systems, he has long recognized the need for a current and comprehensive dictionary of computer terminology that would present the term in a simple, understandable manner.

The selection of words for a dictionary inevitably involves a personal choice, and one has to balance a desire to be comprehensive against the need to be concise. The task of preparing this dictionary involved the collection, correlation, and analysis of over 32,000 words, phrases and acronyms used in connection with computers. This large collection of terms was used as a source for preparing this book. The **Computer Dictionary For Everyone** is a glossary of about 2500 words, phrases, and acronyms used in connection with computers.

Special features of the book include:

COMPUTER ORGANIZATIONS Short descriptions are given to acquaint the reader with professional organizations such as ACM, DPMA, AEDS, AFIPS, BEMA, SPA and IFIPS.

METRIC SYSTEM The USA is going metric - it is essential that everyone learn how to use metric measurements. Important metric terms are defined in this book and metric values are used throughout the book.

BIOGRAPHIES Notes on the life histories of the most important people of computer science. Emphasis is given to their influence on the development of computer techniques and equipment. Examples: Aiken, Atanasoff, Babbage, Boole, Eckert, Hollerith, Leibniz, Mauchly, Napier, Pascal, Turing, von Neumann, Watson, Weiner, and Zuse.

PROGRAMMING LANGUAGES Included in the book are definitions of APL, BASIC, COBOL, COGO, JOVIAL, LOGO, FORTRAN, GPSS, PL/1, RPG, SNOBOL, Tiny BASIC, WATFOR, as well as many other programming languages.

PERSONAL COMPUTERS The recent introduction of microprocessors and microcomputers has led to widespread usage of small computers by practically everyone — students, teachers, engineers, laymen. Users of small computers will find terms such as microcomputer, ROM, RAM, PROM, large scale integration, cross compiling, chip, and floppy disk.

HISTORICAL In addition to short sketches of famous people, the book also includes descriptions of many famous computers. Examples: EDSAC, EDVAC, ENIAC, MARK I, and UNIVAC I.

COMPUTERS IN SOCIETY The reader is made aware of the effects of computers on society by reading the definition of terms such as cashless society, personal computer, and microprocessor.

MANAGEMENT Businessmen will find terms to aid them in their everyday activities. Examples: centralized data processing, computer security, data base, distributed data processing, feasibility study, information retrieval, and management information system.

EDUCATION Computers are now being used in all aspects of education — administrative and instructional. Teachers will find descriptions for acronyms such as BASIC, CAI, CAL, CMI, CRT, CPU, EDP, I/O, MICR, OCR, PLATO, and TICCIT.

COMPUTER PROFESSIONALS Programmers and analysts will find many useful terms. Examples: algorithm, byte, data base, heuristic, intelligent terminals, laser storage, multiprocessing, operating system, point-of-sale terminal, simulation, structured programming, time-sharing and virtual storage.

I am particularly indebted to my wife, Rae, for her help with this book; and to Robert Cameron and Charles Pike, Daytona Beach Community College, and Robert Aumiller, General Electric Company, who kindly consented to read and make comments about the book. Finally, I should like to express the hope that readers who find the mistakes and omissions which undoubtedly remain, will be so kind as to let me know, so they may be corrected in future editions.

Ormond Beach, Florida   Donald D. Spencer

CONTENTS

INTRODUCTION
TO
COMPUTERS

Computers are having a profound effect on today's society. Their effects on the day-to-day lives of nearly everyone are greater than many persons realize. In short, the computer is becoming so essential a tool, with so much potential for changing our lives and our world, that most people should know something about it.

Computers have radically altered the world of business. Almost all utility bills, telephone bills and bank statements are calculated and produced by computers. They have affected military strategy, increased human productivity, made many products less expensive, and lowered barriers to knowledge. They have opened new horizons to the fields of science and medicine, improved the efficiency of government, and changed the techniques of education.

Did you also realize that the television program you watch may be following a computer-generated plan and that the pies and cakes you eat may have the quantity of ingredients controlled by a computer?

Computers route long-distance telephone calls, help design airplanes and automobiles, prepare weather forecasts, check income tax returns, direct traffic in large cities, compose music, play games, grade test papers, reserve seats of an airplane, diagnose patients, schedule classes and control microwave ovens.

Computers can store every variety of information that humans record and almost instantly recall it for use. They can calculate tens of millions of times faster than the brain and can solve in seconds many problems that would take batteries of experts years to complete. Computers have given science and technology the greatest tool ever developed for turning the forces of nature to human use.

Computer technology has improved at a tremendously fast pace during the past three decades. During the past few years alone computers have become much smaller, faster, and less expensive to purchase and operate. When computers were originally developed, many thought that only a few large businesses would use them; they were seen as too powerful, costly, and complicated for most concerns. Today elementary school children use classroom microcomputers to help them learn arithmetic and language skills.

The early computers were built with thousands of *vacuum tubes*. Walking into a computer room in the 1950s was a "chilly" experience, because the room was very cool, almost cold, in fact. Vacuum tubes gave off a considerable amount of heat, and keeping the machine cool required that it be operated in an air conditioned room.

By the early 1960s, the vacuum tube was replaced by the transistor. *Transistors* are much smaller and more efficient in their use of energy than vacuum tubes are. The use of transistors greatly increased the reliability of computers. The use of transistor components resulted in much less hardware maintenance, thereby greatly reducing the cost of operating a computer system. The speed of computers using transistors was measured in microseconds, a factor of 1000 times faster than the speed of vacuum tube machines.

Another major advance came with the introduction of the *integrated circuit*. Instead of using individual transistors and wiring them together into a circuit, it became possible to etch all the components and all the connections required for the circuit on a small piece of silicon by using photographic techniques. By using integrated circuits, computer manufacturers were able to produce machines that were smaller, less expensive, and more reliable.

Today, integrated circuit chips are being made that contain a complete computer on a silicon chip only 6.4mm (¼ of an inch) square (called a *computer-on-a-chip*). With large scale integrated circuitry, the trend of falling computer size and prices has continued very dramatically. Today, one can purchase a computer for only a few hundred dollars that is a thousand times more powerful than one of the early vacuum tube machines, which cost several hundred thousand dollars.

Computer systems vary considerably in size and complexity; however, they are all similar in many ways. Each computer system must be able to *read in* instructions and data, *remember* the problem being solved and the data to use, *perform calculations* (and other manipulations) on the data, *print out* the results, and *control* the entire operation.

Two needed elements of computer processing are input data and a program. *Input data* is the information to be processed. This data might be contained in sales slips, census statistics, inventory reports, purchase orders, employee time-cards, medical reports, invoices, or some other record. A *program* is a set of instructions a computer follows in processing the data.

The program and data are fed into the computer's storage through an *input device*. The *central processing unit* (CPU), which is the processing and control part of a computer system, manipulates the data according to the program instructions. The processed data, or answer is produced on an *output device*.

Input and output devices are the means by which the computer communicates with the outside world. The *display terminal* is used widely as a computer input/output device. This device looks like a cross between a typewriter and a TV set. Information sent from the computer to the terminal is displayed on the screen. The terminal keyboard is used to give this device a two-way communications capability.

The *typewriter*, which may be used as a keyboard input device as well as an output printing device, provides a method for printing limited amounts of information. The *line printer* is an output device that prints information at a very fast rate.

Automatic plotting devices are used with computers to produce pictorial or graphic representations of information. The *digital plotter* is a device that can draw under control of the computer. Typical applications might be the drawing of graphs, weather maps, building plans, or computerized art.

Point-of-sale terminals are becoming rather commonplace in department stores and supermarkets. These terminals are connected to a computer and are used to automate the sales function as well as provide a perpetual inventory control system.

Other input/output devices are *card readers* and *punches, paper tape readers* and *punches, magnetic-ink character readers, optical readers, microfilm units,* and *audio response terminals.*

The capability of a computer to "remember" is one of its fundamental and most essential facilities. It would be impossible for a computer to operate without its having some way of storing instructions, facts, and figures for retrieval when needed. *Computer storage* is actually an electronic file where instructions and data are retained as long as they are required. Computer storage is divided into two classes: internal storage and auxiliary storage. *Internal storage* is the specific storage unit that serves the central processing unit. It is the main storage of the computer. The internal storage of most computers is composed of either *integrated circuit chips* or *magnetic cores*. *Bubble memory chips* are also beginning to be used in some of the newer computers. *Auxiliary storage* is used to supplement the main storage of a computer. Common auxiliary storage devices are *disk units, floppy disk units, magnetic tape units,* and *cassette tape units.*

Computers can provide outstanding results. But, because they do only what they are instructed to do, some form of communication must exist between them and the persons who use them. In other words, they must be programmed. Without a program, a computer is a helpless collection of electronic circuitry. With a proper program, a computer can play chess, guide a space vehicle to a distant planet, or do one of numerous other tasks.

A computer does not do any thinking and cannot make unplanned decisions. Every step of each problem it handles has to be accounted for by a program. If a problem requires intuition or guessing, or is so hard to define that it cannot be put into precise words, the computer cannot solve it. A great deal of thought must be put into defining the problem exactly and setting it up for the computer in such a way that every possible alternative is taken care of. You should remember that computers are used to implement solutions to problems. Computers do not solve problems; *people solve problems.* The computer carries out the solution as specified by people.

There are five steps involved in the solution of a problem with a computer:

1. Problem definition
2. Flowcharting
3. Writing the program
4. Testing the program
5. Documentation

Problem definition is the process of defining "exactly" what the problem is before attempting to solve it. Generally, a problem can be considered defined when all inputs and outputs have been identified, when the outputs have been determined to be correct, and a solution to the problem can be flowcharted or represented in a step-by-step form.

A *flowchart* is a drawing which helps to display the logic used to solve a problem. It is composed of a sequence of special symbols connected by straight lines. Flowcharts are an excellent method for expressing what you want a computer to do.

Coding is the name given to the writing of instructions for a sequence of computer operations. Normally, one uses a flowchart to code a program. The program is written in a programming language. *Programming languages* provide the common communication link between computers and people. Programming languages such as BASIC, FORTRAN, COBOL, APL, and PL/I permit people to write computer instructions in near-human languages.

After the program has been translated into a language that the computer understands, it is necessary to execute the program on the computer to determine if it works properly, and, if not, to make the required program revisions to make it do so. This step is called *program debugging* or "testing the program."

After the program is working, a *documentation package* should be put together which will help other people use the program. *Software* is a general term that applies to everything other than *hardware* that is used in a computer system. One usually thinks of software as being the instructions that direct the operation of a computer, plus the various paper documents detailing the proper use of the instructions.

Computer science is one of several information handling technologies. Important advancements have preceded computers and, probably, others will follow. Though many persons take for granted earlier information developments - photography, printing, the telephone, radio and television - each has had a marked influence on society. Computers, too, will some day be taken for granted. As an understanding of them becomes more widespread, their capabilities will seem less and less amazing, though their total influence probably will continue to increase.

ORGANIZATION
AND
USAGE

Most terms appear in alphabetical order rather than under a general heading. For example, **floppy disk** and **moveable-head disk unit** appear under F and M, though they are mentioned and cross referenced under the general description of **magnetic disk.**

Cross references that are important to an understanding of any term are usually given in *italics.* If you are unfamiliar with descriptions of modern computer terms, it might be helpful to begin by looking up some of these words which appear over and over again, though not always as cross references.

assembler	microcomputer
binary	microprocessor
cathode ray tube	object program
central processing unit	off-line
compiler	on-line
computer	output
data	program
debug	programming language
digital	PROM
EPROM	RAM
flowchart	ROM
hardware	simulation
input	software
instruction	source program
loop	symbolic programming
machine language	terminal

If you cannot find a word, it might be listed in a slightly different form. For example, you might try looking for "flowcharting" and find your description under "flowchart".

DICTIONARY
OF
TERMS

A

abacus An ancient device for doing simple calculations, using movable beads threaded on a grid of wires.

ABC An acronym for Atanasoff-Berry Computer. An early electronic digital computer built in 1942 by Dr. John V. Atanasoff, and his assistant, Clifford Berry.

absolute address An address that is permanently assigned by the machine designer to a particular storage location. For example, the addresses, 0000, 0001, 0002, and 0003 might be assigned to the first four locations in a computer's storage. Also called *machine address.*

absolute coding Coding that uses machine instructions and absolute addresses; therefore, it can be directly executed by a computer without prior translation to a different form. Contrast with *symbolic coding.*

absolute value The magnitude of a number without regard to sign.

abstract A summary of a document.

AC An acronym for *Automatic Computer.*

acceptance test A test used to demonstrate the capabilities and workability of a new computer system. It is usually conducted by the manufacturer to show the customer that the system is in working order.

access arm A mechanical device on a disk file storage unit which positions the reading and writing mechanism.

access method Any of the data management techniques available to the user for transferring data between internal storage and an input/output device.

access time The time interval between the instant data are called for from the storage unit and the instant data are delivered (read time). The time interval between the instant data are requested to be stored and the instant at which storage is completed (write time). See also *transfer rate.*

accounting machine A keyboard activated machine used to prepare printed reports from punch-card data. The machine can also perform limited arithmetic operations.

accumulator A register or storage location that forms the result of an arithmetic or logic operation.

accuracy The degree of exactness of an approximation or measurement. Accuracy normally denotes absolute quality of computed results; *precision* usually refers to the amount of detail used in representing those results. Thus, four-place results are less precise than six-place results; nevertheless a four-place table might be more accurate than an erroneously computed six-place table. See *precision*.

ACM An acronym for Association for Computing Machinery. A professional computer science organization. Its function is to advance the design, development, and application of information processing and the interchange of such techniques between computer specialists and users.

acoustic coupler A modem which converts data' to be transmitted into a sequence of different tones which are sent via a conventional telephone handset to a receiving modem which converts them back to a stream of binary digits.

ACPA An acronym for Association of Computer Programmer and Analysts. A professional computer science organization.

acronym A word formed from the first letter (or letters) of the words in a phrase or name; e.g., BASIC from Beginner's All-purpose Symbolic Instruction Code, RPG from Report Program Generator, CPU from Central Processing Unit.

action (1) The performance of a particular operation or set of operations in response to a stimulus. (2) The resulting activity of a given condition.

activity A term to indicate that a record in a master file is used, altered, or referred to.

activity ratio When a file is processed, the ratio of the number of records in a file which have activity to the total number of records in that file.

ADAPSO An acronym for Association of Data Processing Service Organizations. An association of commercial institutions. ADAPSO offers data-processing services through systems its members operate on their own premises.

adaptive systems Systems displaying the ability to learn, change their state, or otherwise react to a stimulus. Any system capable of adapting itself to changes in its environment.

add time The time required for a computer to perform an addition, exclusive of the time required to obtain the quantities from storage and put the sum back into storage.

addend A number of quantity to be added to another, the augend, to obtain a result called the sum.

adder A device capable of forming the sum of two or more quantities. See *parallel adder* and *serial adder*.

adding wheel A toothed gear which allows "carrying" to be accomplished mechanically. Adding wheels were used in Blaise Pascal's adding machine and many later calculating devices.

address An identification (e.g., a label, number, or name) that designates a particular location in storage or any other data destination or source.

addition record A record which results from the creation of a new record during the processing of a file.

address modification An operation that causes an address to be altered in a prescribed way by a stored program computer.

address register A register containing the address of the instruction currently being executed.

administrative data processing The field of data processing concerned with the management or direction of an organization.

ADP An acronym for Automatic Data Processing. Data processing performed largely by automatic means.

AEDS An acronym for Association for Educational Data Systems. A professional organization interested in sharing information related to the effect of data processing on the educational process.

AFIPS An acronym for American Federation of Information Processing Societies. A society whose primary purpose is to advance understanding and knowledge of the information processing sciences through active engagement in various scientific activities and cooperation with state, national, and international (called *IFIPS*) organizations on information processing.

Aiken, Howard Headed the team of people who designed and built the first electromechanical computer, the Automatic Sequence Controlled Calculator (commonly called the Mark I), at Harvard University.

23

airline reservation system An on-line direct access application in which a computing system is used to keep track of seat inventories, flight schedules, and other information required to run an airline. The reservation system is designed to maintain up-to-date data files and to respond, within seconds or less, to inquiries from ticket agents at locations remote from the computing system.

algebra The study of mathematical structure. Elementary algebra is the study of numeral systems and their properties. Algebra solves problems in arithmetic by using letters or symbols to stand for quantities.

ALGOL An acronym for ALGOrithmic Language – an international higher-level programming language designed for scientific programming. ALGOL is not widely used in the United States but is popular in Europe.

algorithm A set of well-defined rules for solving a problem in a finite number of steps. Contrast with *heuristic*.

allocate To assign a resource for use in performing a specific job.

allocation The process of reserving computer storage areas for instructions or data.

alphabetic Pertaining to a character set that includes the letters of the alphabet.

alphanumeric A general term for alphabetic letters (A through Z), numerical digits (0 through 9), and special characters (–, /, *, $, (,), +, etc.) which are machine-processable.

alphameric A contraction of alphanumeric.

alteration switch An actual switch on the computer console or a program-simulated switch which can be set on or off to control coded machine instructions.

alternate routing Assignment of a secondary communications path to a destination if the primary path is unavailable.

ALU Abbreviation for Arithmetic Logic Unit. A computational subsystem that performs the mathematical and logical operations of a digital system. A basic element of a central processing unit (CPU). Same as *arithmetic unit*.

ambient temperature The temperature of the environment surrounding an element of a computer system.

amplifier An electronic circuit which increases the voltage, current, or power of an input signal, or isolates one part of a system from another.

ampere Base unit of electric current in the SI metric system.

analog Pertaining to representation by means of continuously variable physical quantities. The spelling in Great Britain is analogue. Contrast with *digital*.

analog channel A channel on which the information transmitted can take any value between the defined limits of the channel.

analog computer A computer in which analog representations of data are mainly used. For example, voltages or currents might be used to represent the variables in a differential equation to be solved by an analog computer. See *computer*.

analog data A physical representation of information such that the representation bears an exact relationship to the original information, e.g., the electrical signals on a telephone channel are analog data representation of the original voice data.

analog model A model that relates physical similarity to the actual situation.

analog-to-digital converter Mechanical or electrical devices used to convert continuous analog signals to discrete digital numbers. Abbreviated A-D converter. Opposite of *digital-to-analog converter*. See *digitize*.

analysis The investigation of a problem by some consistent, systematic procedure. See *systems analysis*.

analyst A person skilled in the definition of and the development of techniques for the solving of a problem, especially those techniques for solutions on a computer. See *programming analyst* and *systems analyst*.

analytical engine A device invented in the mid 1800's by Charles Babbage, a British mathematician, to solve mathematical problems. This machine was a forerunner of the modern digital computer.

AND A logical connection, as in the statement A AND B, which means that the statement is true if, and only if, A is true and B is true simultaneously.

AND-gate A computer circuit having two switches in which the output is a binary one only if both inputs are one.

annotation A description or explanation usually in the form of a comment or note.

annotation symbol A flowcharting symbol used to add messages or notes to a flowchart.

ANS An acronym for American National Standards Institute. An organization that acts as a national clearinghouse and coordinator for voluntary standards in the United States.

aperture card A punched card with an opening specifically prepared for the mounting of a frame or frames of microfilm.

APL A mathematically-structured programming language developed by Ken Iverson and Adin Falkoff of IBM Corporation. In its simplest mode of operation, APL performs the functions of an intelligent calculator. The power of the language is demonstrated by its extended single operators which allows a user to directly perform such things as taking the inverse of a matrix, or solving a set of linear equations. APL is a powerful tool to the scientist or engineer.

Apple II A popular microcomputer manufactured by Apple Computer Inc.

application programs The programs normally written by the using organization, that enable the computer to produce useful work. For example, inventory control, attendance accounting, linear programming, medical accounting.

applications programming The preparation of programs for application to specific problems in order to find solutions. Contrast with *systems programming*.

applied mathematics Mathematics put to practical use, as in mechanics, physics, or computer science, among others.

approximation A number that is not exact, but has been rounded off to a prescribed decimal place. An approximation of π is 3.14.

APT An acronym for Automatic Programmed Tool. A programming system which is used in the numerical control applications for programmed control of machine functions. The APT language allows a user to define points, lines, circles, planes, conical surfaces, and geometric surfaces. See *numerical control* and *parts programmer*.

area search The examination of a large group of documents to select those which pertain to one group, such as one category, class, etc.

argument A variable to which either a logical or a numerical value may be assigned.

arithmetic (1) The branch of mathematics concerned with the study of the positive real numbers and zero. (2) Refers to the operations of addition, subtraction, multiplication, and division, or to the section of the computer hardware where these operations are performed. See *arithmetic unit*.

arithmetic operation Various manipulations of numerical quantities, which include the fundamental operations of addition, subtraction, multiplication, and division.

arithmetic shift To multiply or divide a quantity by a power of the number base; for example, if binary 1101, which represents decimal 13, is arithmetically shifted twice to the left, the result is 110100, which represents 52, which is also obtained by multiplying 13 by 2 twice; on the other hand, if the decimal 13 were to be shifted to the left twice, the result would be the same as multiplying by 10 twice, or 1300.

arithmetic unit The portion of the central processing unit where arithmetic and logical operations are performed.

arithmetic-logic unit Same as *arithmetic unit*.

arrangement Order of index terms or items of data in a system.

array (1) A series of related items. (2) An ordered arrangement or pattern of items or numbers, such as a determinant, matrix, vector, or a table of numbers.

artificial intelligence The branch of computer science concerned with the study of, the possibility of, methods of, and implications of developing computer systems which can perform intelligent-like tasks such as interacting in a natural language, game playing, question answering, theorem proving, etc. See *heuristic* and *machine learning*.

artificial language A language based on a set of prescribed rules that are established prior to its usage. Contrast with *natural language*.

ASA An acronym for American Standards Association. Replaced by *ANS*.

ASCC An acronym for Automatic Sequence Controlled Calculator. First electromechanical computer developed under the direction of Howard Aiken at Harvard University. Also called the *Mark I.*

ASCII An acronym for American Standard Code for Information Interchange. A 7-bit (or 8-bit compatible) standard code adopted to facilitate the interchange of data among various types of data processing and data communications equipment.

ascending Increasing. In $x^1+x^2+x^3+x^4$, the exponents are in ascending order.

ASR An acronym for Automatic Send/Receive. A teletypewriter with keyboard, printer, paper tape reader and paper tape punch, which allows tape to be produced and edited off line for automatic transmission. A popular input/output unit for minicomputers, personal computers, and remote time sharing terminals.

assemble To gather, interpret, and coordinate data required for a computer program, translate the data into computer language, and project it into the final program for the computer to follow.

assembler A computer program that takes nonmachine language instructions prepared by a computer user and converts them into a form that may be used by the computer.

assembling The automatic process by which a computer converts a symbolic source language program into a machine language usually on an instruction-by-instruction basis. See *cross compiling/assembling.*

assembly language A programming language which allows a computer user to write a program using mnemonics instead of numeric instructions. It is a low-level symbolic programming language which closely resembles machine code language. Contrast with *problem-oriented language* and *procedure-oriented language.*

assembly listing A listing of the details of an assembly procedure.

associative memory A storage device whose storage locations are identified by their contents (rather than by names or positions, as in most computer storage devices). Same as *content-addressable memory* and *search memory.*

asychronous computer A computer in which each operation starts as a result of a signal generated by the completion of the previous operation or by the availability of the equipment required for the next operation. Contrast with *synchronous computer.*

asynchronous input Input data having no time dependable pattern or cycle when related to the computer system.

asynchronous transmission Transmission of data that requires the use of start and stop elements for each character, because the interval of time between characters can vary.

Atanasoff, John V. Designed an electronic digital computer in 1942. See *ABC.*

ATOLL An acronym for Acceptance Test Or Launch Language. A programming language used for checkout applications on the Apollo launch vehicle.

atom The elementary building block of data structures. An atom corresponds to a record in a file and may contain one or more fields of data. Also called node.

attenuation The decrease in the strength of a signal as it passes through a control system. Opposite of *gain.*

attribute A word that describes the manner in which a variable is handled by the computer.

audio response device An output device that produces a spoken response. See *voice output.*

audio-visual Non-print materials such as films, tapes, cassettes, and other media that record information by sound and sight.

audit trail A means for identifying the actions taken in processing input data or in preparing an output. By use of the audit trail, data on a source document can be traced to an output, and an output can be traced to the source items from which it was derived.

augend A quantity which is added to another quantity.

authors People who design instructional material for *computer-assisted instruction* (CAI) systems.

auto-index To prepare an index by a machine method.

autochart A type of documentor used for the automatic production and maintenance of charts, principally flowcharts.

automatic Pertaining to a process or device that, under specified conditions, functions without intervention by a human operator.

automatic carriage See *carriage*.

automatic check An equipment check built in specifically for checking purposes. Also called *built-in check*.

automatic coding See *automatic programming*.

automatic computer A computer that can process a specified volume of work, its assigned function, without requiring human intervention, except for program changes. See *computer*.

automatic controller A device or instrument which is capable of measuring and regulating by receiving a signal from a sensing device, comparing this data with a desired value and issuing signals for corrective action.

automatic data processing See *data processing*.

automatic error correction A technique for detecting and correcting errors that occur in data transmission or occur within the system itself.

automatic message switching See *message switching*.

automatic programming (1)The process of using a computer to perform some stages of the work involved in preparing a program. (2) The production of a machine-language computer program under the guidance of a symbolic representation of the program.

automatic quality control Technique for evaluating the quality of a product being processed by checking it against a predetermined standard, and automatically making the proper corrective action if the quality falls below the standard.

Automatic Sequence Controlled Calculator See *ASCC*.

automation (1) The implementation of processes by automatic means. (2) Automatically controlled operation of an apparatus, process or system by mechanical or electronic devices that take the place of human observation, effort and decision.

automaton A machine designed to simulate the operations of living things.

auxiliary equipment Equipment not under direct control of the central processing unit. See *off-line*.

auxiliary function In automatic machine tool control, a machine function other than the control of the motion of a work-piece or cutter. Control of machine lubricating and cooling equipment are typical auxiliary functions.

auxiliary memory See *auxiliary storage*.

auxiliary operation An operation performed by equipment not under control of the central processing unit. See *off-line*.

auxiliary storage A storage that supplements the primary internal storage of a computer. Same as *secondary storage*.

availability The ratio of the time that a hardware device is known or believed to be operating correctly to the total hours of scheduled operation. Often called *operating ratio*.

available time (1) The time that a computer is available for use.

B

Babbage, Charles (1792—1871) A British mathematician and inventor. He designed a "difference engine" for calculating logarithms to 20 decimal places and an "analytical engine" that was a forerunner of the digital computer. Babbage was a man ahead of his time, and engineering techniques of his day were not advanced enough to successfully build his machines.

background processing The execution of lower-priority computer programs during periods when the system resources are not required to process higher-priority programs. See *background program*.

background program A program that can be executed whenever the facilities of a multiprogramming computer system are not required by other programs of higher priority. Contrast with *foreground program*.

31

backlash In a mechanical operation, the "play" between interacting parts, such as two gears, as a result of tolerance.

backspace tape The process of returning a magnetic tape to the beginning of the preceding record.

backup Pertaining to procedures or equipment that are available for use in the event of failure or overloading of the normally used equipment or procedures.

Backus normal form A language used for describing languages.

backward read A feature available on some magnetic tape systems whereby the magnetic tape units can transfer data to computer storage while moving in a reverse direction.

badge reader A terminal equipped to read credit cards or specially coded badges.

band (1) In communications, a range of frequencies, as between two specified limits. (2) Range, or scope of operation. (3) A group of circular recording tracks on a storage device such as a disk or drum.

bandwidth In data communications, the difference (expressed in Hertz) between the highest and lowest frequencies of a band.

bank A unit of *internal storage*.

bar printer A printing device that uses several type bars positioned side by side across the line.

base The radix of a number system. See *radix*.

base address A specified address which is combined with a relative address to form the absolute address of a particular storage location.

BASIC An acronym for Beginner's All-purpose Symbolic Instruction Code. An easy-to-learn, easy-to-use, algebraic programming language. BASIC is especially adapted for use on minicomputers or time sharing systems. It is well suited for use in writing programs of modest complexity in scientific, in business and in most other application areas. See *Tiny BASIC*.

basic linkage A linkage which is used repeatedly in one routine, program, or system and which follows the same set of rules each time. See *calling sequence* and *linkage*.

batch A group of records or programs that is considered as a single unit for processing on a computer.

Keyboard-display terminals are used in many systems wherever information is gathered or communicated. With one keystroke, for example, an important report or information item can be called to the screen of the terminal. The terminal is also used to add to or change the information stored in the data base of the computerized information system.

batch processing A technique by which programs that are to be executed are coded and collected together into groups for processing in groups or batches. The user gives his job to a computer center, it is put in a batch of programs, processed and data returned. The user has no direct access to the machine. See *remote batch processing*.

batch total A sum of a set of items in a batch of records which is used to check the accuracy of operations involving the batch.

Batten system A method of indexing invented by W. E. Batten, utilizing the coordination of single attributes to identify specific documents. Sometimes called the "peek-a-boo" system because of its method of comparing holes in cards by super-imposing cards and checking the coincidence of holes.

baud A unit for expressing the speed of transmitting data over distances. One baud is one bit per second.

Baudot code A code for the transmission of data in which five bits represent one character. It is named for Emile Baudot, a pioneer in printing telegraphy. The name is usually applied to the code used in many teleprinter systems.

BCD An acronym for Binary Coded Decimal.

BEMA An acronym for Business Equipment Manufacturers Association. An organization whose main function is to guide information processing equipment users in solving problems and applying information for general benefit, and to sponsor the settings of standards for computers and information processing.

benchmark problem A problem used to evaluate the performance of digital computers relative to each other.

benchmarking The use of a point of reference against which measurements can be made, as the use of a program to evaluate the performance of a computer.

bias The amount by which the average of a set of values departs from a reference value.

bibliography (1) An annotated catalog of documents. (2) An enumerative list of books. (3) A list of documents pertaining to a given subject or author. (4) The process of compiling catalogs or lists.

bifurcation A condition where two, and only two outcomes can occur; e.g., on or off, 0 or 1.

BINAC An acronym for BINary Automatic Computer. Built by the Eckert-Mauchly Corporation in 1949.

binary Pertaining to the number system with a radix of 2, or to a characteristic or property involving a choice or condition in which there are two possibilities.

binary arithmetic A mathematical numeration system equivalent to our decimal arithmetic system but involving only two digits: one and zero.

binary code A coding system in which the encoding of any data is done through the use of bits — that is, 0 or 1.

binary coded character One element of a notation system representing alphameric characters such as decimal digits, alphabetic letters, and special symbols by a predetermined configuration of consecutive binary digits.

binary coded decimal A computer coding system in which each decimal digit is represented by a group of four binary ones and zeros. Abbreviated BCD.

binary coded decimal number A number usually consisting of successive groups of figures, in which each group of four figures is a binary number that represents but does not necessarily equal arithmetically, a particular figure in an associated decimal number; for example, the decimal number 264 is represented as the binary coded number 0010 0110 0100.

binary device (1) A device that can register two conditions; e.g., an electrical switch which can be ON or OFF. (2) In computer science, equipment that records data in binary form or that reads the data so coded.

binary digit Either of the characters 0 or 1. Abbreviated "bit."

binary notation A numeral system written in base two notation.

binary system A numeral system with a base or radix of two; e.g., the numeral 111 represents the quantity 1, plus 1×2^1, plus 1×2^2 — i.e., 7.

binary point The radix point in the binary numeral. The point that separates the fractional part of a mixed binary numeral from the integer part. In the binary numeral 110.011, the binary point is between the two zeros.

binary search A search in which the series of items is divided into two parts, one of which is rejected, and the process repeated on the unrejected part until the item with the desired property is found. Also known as *dichotomizing search*.

binary-to-decimal conversion The process of converting a numeral written to the base two to the equivalent numeral written to the base ten.

binary-to-gray code conversion A gray code equivalent of a binary numeral can be obtained by applying the following rule: The most significant gray code digit equals the corresponding binary digit and the following gray code digit is 1 if the binary digit changes and 0 if it does not. For example, the binary value 0110100 equals the gray code value 0101110.

binary-to-hexadecimal conversion The process of converting a numeral written to the base two to the equivalent numeral written to the base sixteen.

binary-to-octal conversion The process of converting a numeral written to the base two to the equivalent numeral written to the base eight.

bionics The study of living systems, for the purpose of relating their characteristics and functions to the development of mechanical and electronic hardware (hardware systems).

bipolar The most popular fundamental kind of integrated circuit, formed from layers of silicon with different electrical characteristics. Bipolar literally means "having two poles" and is used to distinguish the earlier transistor from the MOS Field Effect Transistor (MOSFET), which is unipolar (having one pole). As in MOSFET, the current flow of majority carriers is in one direction only - for example, from source to drain. In a bipolar transistor, the current in the emitter region splits and flows toward two terminals (poles), the base and the collector.

biquinary code A 7-bit weighted code used primarily to represent decimal numbers. It is a redundant code which may be utilized to provide error-checking features. A pair of bits represents the decimal number 5 or 0, and the remaining five bits are used to represent the decimal numbers 0 through 4.

bistable device A device with only two stable states, such as *on* and *off*.

bit A binary digit; a digit (1 or 0) in the representation of a number in binary notation.

bit density A measure of the number of bits recorded per unit of length or area.

bit rate The rate at which binary digits, or pulse representations, appear on communication lines or channels.

bit stream Referring to a binary signal without regard to groupings by character.

BIZMAC An acronym for Business Machine Computer. An early, large computer that was installed at the Ordnance Tank-Automotive Command in Detroit, Michigan.

black box An electronic or mechanical device which alters input signals in a predictable manner but whose inner workings are often a mystery to the user.

blank character A character used to produce a character space on an output medium.

block A group of digits, characters, or words that are held in one section of an input/output medium and handled as a unit, e.g., the data recorded between two interblock gaps on a magnetic tape. See *input block* and *output block*.

block diagram A graphic representation showing the logical sequence by which data is processed. See *flowchart.*

block length A measure of the size of a block, usually specified in units such as records, words, characters, or bytes.

block sorting A sorting technique used to break down a file into related groups.

blocking Combining two or more records into one block usually to increase the efficiency of computer input and output operations.

blocking factor The number of logical records per physical record on a magnetic tape or disk.

BNF An acronym for Backus Naur Form. A notation for describing the syntax of programming languages.

bookkeeping Same as *housekeeping.*

Boole, George (1815-1864) The father of Boolean algebra. A British logician and mathematician. In 1847, he wrote a pamphlet called "Mathematical Analysis of Logic." In 1851, he wrote a more mature statement of his logical system in a larger work, "An Investigation of the Laws of Thought," in which are founded the mathematical theories of logic. Boolean algebra lay dormant until its useful application to the field of relay switching and electronic computers. It has now become an important subject to logic design of electronic computers.

Boolean algebra A branch of symbolic logic which is similar in form to algebra but, instead of numerical relationships, it deals with logical relationships. An algebra named for *George Boole.*

Boolean operator A logic operator each of whose operands and whose result have one of two values.

bootstrap loader A technique for loading the first few instructions of a routine into storage, then using these instructions to bring in the rest of the routine. This usually involves either the entering of a few instructions manually or by activating a special switch on the computer console which causes the execution of a hardware bootstrap program.

bore Inside diameter of the hub on a magnetic tape reel.

borrow An arithmetically negative carry. It occurs in direct subtraction by raising the low order digit of the minuend by one unit of the next higher order digit.

bpi An abbreviation for bits per inch or bytes per inch; e.g., magnetic tape can have 1600 bpi.

bps An abbreviation for bits per second or bytes per second.

branch The selection of one or more possible paths in the flow of control, based on some criterion. See *conditional transfer, jump,* and *unconditional transfer.*

branch instruction An instruction to a computer that enables one to instruct the computer to choose between alternative program paths depending upon the conditions determined by the computer during the execution of the program.

breadboard Usually refers to an experimental or rough construction model of a process, device, or construction.

breakpoint A specified point in a program at which the program may be interrupted by manual intervention or by a control routine. Breakpoints are generally used as an aid in testing and debugging programs.

broad-band As applied to data communications, used to denote transmission facilities capable of handling frequencies greater than those required for high-grade voice communications.

broadcast In data communications, the dissemination of information to a number of stations simultaneously.

brute-force technique Any mathematical technique that depends on the raw power of a computer to arrive at a non-elegant solution of a mathematical problem. Most computer users try to avoid brute-force techniques unless there is no practical alternate.

bubble memory See *magnetic bubble memory.*

bucket A term used to indicate a specific portion of storage.

buffer A temporary storage area which is used to equalize or balance the different operating speeds. For example, a buffer can be used between a slow input device, such as a typewriter, and the main computer which operates at a very high speed.

buffered computer A computer which provides for simultaneous input/output and process operations.

bug A term used to denote a mistake in a computer program or system, or a malfunction in a computer hardware component. Hence debugging — removing mistakes and correcting malfunctions. See *malfunction* and *mistake*.

built-in check See *automatic check*.

burst mode A method of reading or writing data that does not permit an interrupt to occur.

bus A channel or path for transferring data and electrical signals.

business applications Computer systems involving normal day-to-day accounting procedures such as payroll, accounts receivable, accounts payable, and inventory.

business data processing Data processing for business purposes, e.g., payroll, scheduling, accounting.

business programming A branch of computer programming in which business problems are coded for computer solution. Business programming usually involves relatively few calculations with a large number of data inputs and outputs. See *business applications*.

byte (1) A grouping of adjacent binary digits operated on by the computer as a unit. The most common size byte contains eight binary digits. (2) A group of binary digits used to encode a single character.

C

cache memory An ultra high speed storage module used for input/output or portions of a program requiring high speed execution.

cage A chassis in which printed circuit cards are mounted.

CAI An acronym for *Computer-Assisted Instruction*.

CAI authors See *authors*.

CAL An acronym for *Computer-Augmented Learning*.

calculating Reconstructing or creating new data by compressing certain numeric facts.

calculating punch A machine designed to perform arithmetic operations with punch cards.

calculator Any mechanical or electronic machine used for performing calculations. Calculators, as distinguished from computers, usually require more-or-less continuous human intervention. See *calculating punch*, and *hand calculator.*

call (1) To transfer control to a specific closed subroutine. (2) In communications, the action performed by the calling party, or the operations necessary in making a call, or the effective use made of a connection between two stations. Synonymous with *cue.*

calling sequence A specified set of instructions and data necessary to call a given subroutine.

CAM An acronym for Computer Aided Manufacturing.

canned routines Routines which are coded by the manufacturer and supplied to the user in a machine-readable form.

capacity See *storage capacity.*

capstan The rotating shaft within a magnetic tape drive which pulls the tape across the recording heads at a constant speed.

card A storage medium in which data is represented by means of holes punched in vertical columns in a 18.7 cm by 8.3 cm (7⅜ inches by 3¼) paper card. See *Hollerith card, punched card, ninety-six column card.*

card code The combinations of punched holes which represent characters in a punch card. See *Hollerith code.*

card column One of the vertical lines of punching positions on a punch card.

card deck A set of punch cards.

card face The printed side of a punch card.

card feed A mechanism which moves cards into a machine one at a time.

card field A fixed number of consecutive card columns assigned to a unit of information.

card hopper A device that holds cards and makes them

available for the feeding mechanism of card handling equipment.

card image A representation in storage of the holes punched in a card.

card punch An output device which accepts information from the computer's memory and punches it into cards. A keyboard device by which an operator can punch cards, also known as a *keypunch*.

card punching See *keypunching*.

card reader An input device which reads information punched into cards. The information read is transferred into the computer's memory.

card reproducer A device that reproduces a punch card by punching a similar card. See *reproducing punch*.

card row One of the horizontal lines of punching positions on a punch card.

card stacker The receptacle into which cards are accumulated after passing through a punch-card data processing machine.

card sorting Separating a deck of punch cards into stacks in accordance with the holes punched into the individual cards.

card-to-disk converter A device which converts data directly from punch cards to disk storage.

card-to-tape converter A device which converts data directly from punch cards to magnetic or paper tape.

card verification A means of checking the accuracy of keypunching. A second operator verifies the original punching by depressing the keys of a verifier while reading the same source data. The machine compares the key depressed with the hole already punched in the card, and if they are not identical, indicates an error.

caret A symbol used to indicate the location of the **radix** point of a number. See *radix point*.

carriage A control mechanism for a typewriter or printer that automatically feeds, skips, spaces, or ejects paper forms.

carriage control tape A tape that is punched with the information that is needed to control line feeding on a *line printer*.

carriage return In a character-by-character printing mechanism, the operation that causes the next character to be printed at the left margin. Abbreviated CR.

carry A process of bringing forward. The carry digit or the digit which is to be added to the next higher column, or a special condition which occurs when the sum of two digits in a single column is equal to or greater than the numbering base.

cartridge See *magnetic tape cartridge.*

cascade control An automatic control system in which the control units are linked chain-fashion, each feeding into (and regulating) the next stage.

cashless society A conceptual computerized system in which credit transactions would be settled instantaneously by transferring credits from the customer's bank account to the store's account via a point-of-sale terminal.

cassette See *magnetic tape cassette.*

catalog An ordered compilation of item descriptions and sufficient information to afford access to the items.

catena A connected series.

cathode ray tube An electronic tube with a screen upon which information may be displayed. Abbreviated CRT.

A CRT display unit such as shown above is a popular input/output unit for use with computers.

CBL An acronym for *Computer-Based Learning.*

CDC An acronym for Call Directing Code. Two or three character code used to route automatically a message or command.

cell The storage for one unit of information, usually one character, one byte, or one word. A binary cell is a cell of one binary digit capacity. Also called *storage location.*

celsius Alternate of the kelvin, the base unit of temperature in the SI metric system.

centisecond One hundredth of a second.

centralized data processing A concept where a company has all its computing equipment located at the same site while field-office operations have no effective data processing capability. Contrast with *distributed data processing.*

central information file The main data storage system.

central processing unit The component of a computer system with the circuitry to control the interpretation and execution of instructions. Abbreviated CPU. Synonymous with *central processor* and *main frame.*

central processor See *central processing unit.*

chad A piece of material removed when forming a hole or notch in punched paper tape.

chadded paper Perforated tape with the chad completely removed.

chadless tape Perforated tape with the chad partially removed.

chain Linking of records by means of pointers in such a way that all like records are connected, the last record pointing to the first.

chain field A field in a record which defines the location and storage device of other data items logically related to the original record but not physically attached.

chain printer A line printer in which the type slugs are carried by the links of a revolving chain. See *line printer.*

chaining A process of linking a series of records, programs or operations together.

chaining search A technique for retrieving data from a file by using addresses in the records that link each record to the next in the chain.

43

channel (1) A path for electrical transmission between two or more points. Also called a path, link, line, facility or circuit. (2) A transmission path that connects auxiliary devices to a computer.

channel capacity In data communications, a term used to express the maximum number of bits per second which can be accommodated by a channel. This maximum number is determined by the band width modulation scheme and certain types of noise. The channel capacity is most often measured in bauds or bits per second.

character Any symbol, digit, letter, or punctuation mark stored or processed by computing equipment.

character code A code designating a unique numerical representation for a set of characters.

character density A measure of the number of characters recorded per unit of length or area.

character printer A printer in which only a single character is composed and determined within the device prior to printing.

character reader See *optical character reader*.

character recognition The identification of phonic, graphic, or other characters by automatic means. See *magnetic ink character recognition*, and *optical character recognition*.

character set Comprises the numbers, letters, and symbols associated with a given device or coding system.

character string A string of alphanumeric characters.

characteristic That part of a floating point number which represents the size of the exponent.

charactron A special type of cathode ray tube which displays alphanumeric and special characters on its screen.

chassis The metal base upon which the wiring, sockets, and other electronic parts of an electronic assembly are mounted.

check bit A binary check digit. See also *parity checking*.

check digits One or more digits carried within a unit item of information which provide information about the other digits in the unit in such a manner that if an error occurs, the check fails, and an indication of error is given. See *check bit* and *parity checking*.

check sum A summation of digits or bits used primarily for checking purposes and summed according to an arbitrary set of rules.

checkout See *debug*.

checkpoint A place in a routine where a check is performed.

Chinese-binary code Same as *column-binary code*.

chip (1) A small integrated-circuit package containing many logic elements. A small piece of silicon impregnated with impurities in a pattern to form transistors, diodes, and resistors. Electrical paths are formed on it by depositing thin layers of aluminum or gold. (2) That piece of card removed in punching a hole.

churning See *thrashing*.

circuit A pathway designed for the controlled flow of electrons. A system of conductors and related electrical elements through which electrical currents flow.

circular shift A shifting operation where bits or characters shifted off one end of a register enter the register on the opposite end. Also called *end-around shift*.

CIU See *computer interface unit*.

class A group having the same or similar characteristics.

classify To arrange into classes of information according to a system or method.

clearing Replacing the information in a register, storage location, or storage unit with zeros or blanks.

clock (1) A timing device that generates the basic periodic signal used to control the timing of all operations in a synchronous computer. (2) A device that records the progress of real-time, or some approximation of it, and whose contents are available to a computer program.

closed loop A loop which is completely circular. See *loop*.

closed routine See *closed subroutine*.

closed shop The operation of the data processing center by professional operators. Programs and data are carried by messengers or transmitted over telephone lines, avoiding the necessity of users entering the computer room. This enables a very much more efficient use of the computer, and is opposed to the "open shop" in which each user puts his own program in the machine and fiddles with the switches on the console. Contrast with *open shop.*

closed subroutine A subroutine that can be stored at one place and can be linked to one or more calling routines. Contrast with *open subroutine.*

CMI An acronym for *Computer-Managed Instruction.*

CMOS An acronym for Complementary MOS. A method of making MOS (metallic oxide semiconductor) chips that use almost no power, and are faster than MOS. CMOS is not very good for LSI (large scale integration) but is used in electronic watches and clocks where power has to come from a battery.

COBOL An acronym for COmmon Business Oriented Language — a higher level language developed for business data-processing applications. Every COBOL source program has four divisions, whose names and functions are as follows: (1) Identification Division, which identifies the source program and the output of a compilation, (2) Environment Division, which specifies those aspects of a data processing problem that are dependent upon the physical characteristics of a particular computer, (3) Data Division, which describes the data that the object program is to accept as input, manipulate, create, or produce as output, and (4) Procedure Division which specifies the procedures to be performed by the object program, by means of English-like statements.

CODASYL An acronym for Conference Of DAta SYstem Language. A conference formed to standardize the rules of the COBOL programming language.

code (1) A set of rules outlining the way in which data may be represented. (2) Rules used to convert data from one representation to another. (3) To write a program or routine. (4) Same as *encode.*

code conversion A process for changing the bit groupings for characters in one code into the corresponding character bit groupings for a second code.

code set The complete set of representations defined by a code; e.g., all of the two-letter post office identifications for the 50 states.

coded decimal number A number consisting of successive characters or a group of characters in which each character or group of characters usually represents a specific figure in an associated decimal number.

coder A person whose primary duty is to write (but not design) computer programs.

coding (1) The writing of a list of instructions which will cause a computer to perform specified operations. (2) An ordered list or lists of the successive instructions which will cause a computer to perform a particular process.

coding form A form on which the instructions for programming a computer are written. Also called a *coding sheet*.

coding sheet See *coding form*.

COGO An acronym for COordinate GeOmetry. A problem-oriented programming language used for solving geometric problems. Used primarily by civil engineers.

collate To merge two (or more) sequenced data sets to produce a resulting data set which reflects the sequencing of the original sets. Same as *merge*.

collating sequence An ordering assigned to the characters of a character set to be used for sequencing purposes.

collating sorting A sort which uses a technique of continuous merging of data until one sequence is developed.

collator A machine used to collate or merge sets of cards or other documents into a sequence.

collection See *data collection*.

column (1) The vertical members of one line of an array. (2) One of the vertical lines of punching positions on a punched card. (3) A position of information in a computer word. Contrast with *row*.

column-binary code A code used with punch cards in which successive bits are represented by the presence or absence of punches on contiguous positions in successive columns as opposed to rows. Same as *Chinese-binary code*.

column split A device for distinguishing the pulses corresponding to an 11 or 12 punch from those corresponding to numeric punches in a card column and making them separately available while reading or punching a card.

COM An acronym for Computer Output to Microfilm. See *computer output microfilm recorder*.

47

command (1) A control signal. (2) Loosely, a mathematical or logic operator. (3) Loosely, a computer instruction. See *operation code.*

command processing The reading, analyzing, and performing of computer instructions.

comment cards Verbal messages inserted into a computer program, which do not trigger any computer processing steps but are useful notes to future users who may later attempt to understand or alter the program.

common carrier A company that provides telephone, telegraph, and other telecommunication equipment for public use.

common language A standardized coding procedure common to several different machines; e.g., FORTRAN, COBOL, PL/I. Same as *universal language.*

command chained memory A technique used in dynamic storage allocation.

communication (1) The flow of information from one point (the source) to another (the receiver). (2) The act of transmitting or making known.

communication channel The medium of communication in an electronic telecommunication system. The path through which electrical transmission may take place. Also called *communication link.*

communication link See *communication channel.*

communication satellite An earth orbiting device capable of relaying communication signals over long distances.

compatibility A property of some computers that allows programs written for one computer to run on another (compatible) computer, even though it is a different model. See *family of computers.*

comparator A device for checking the accuracy of transcribed data by comparing it with a second transcription, noting any variation between the two.

compare To examine the representation of a quantity to determine its relationship to zero or to examine two quantities usually for the purposes of determining identity or relative magnitude.

comparison The act of comparing. The common forms are comparison of two numbers for identity, comparison of two numbers for relative magnitude, comparison of two characters for similarity and comparison of the signs of two numbers.

compatible A quality possessed by a computer system which enables it to handle both data and programs devised for some other type of computer system.

compile To prepare a machine language program (or a program expressed in symbolic coding) from a program written in another higher level programming language, such as FORTRAN, PL/I or COBOL.

compile-and-go An operating technique in which the loading and execution phases of a program compilation are performed in one continuous run. This technique is especially useful when a program must be compiled for a one-time application.

compiler A computer program that produces a machine language program from a source program that is usually written in a higher level language by a computer user. The compiler is capable of replacing single source program statements with a series of machine language instructions or with a subroutine.

compiler-compiler Same as *metacompiler*.

compiler language A source language that uses a compiler to translate the language statements into an object language. See *problem-oriented language* and *procedure-oriented language*.

compiler program See *compiler*.

compiling See *compile* and *cross compiling/assembling*.

complement A number used to represent the negative of a given number. A complement is obtained by subtracting each digit of the number from the number representing its base and, in the case of two's and ten's complement, adding unity to the last significant digit.

complex number A number of the form $a+bi$ where a and b are real numbers and i is equal to the square root of minus 1.

component A basic part. An *element*.

composite card A multipurpose data card, or a card that contains data needed in the processing of various applications.

49

compute-bound Programs which have an abundance of computations (compared to the amount of input/output). Contrast with *I/O bound.*

computer A device designed to execute a sequence of mathematical or logical operations automatically, that is without human intervention. Used for the high-speed processing of large volumes of data. See *analog computer, computer kit, digital computer, home computer, microcomputer, minicomputer, microprocessor, personal computer* and *small business computer.*

computer-aided design A process involving direct, real-time communication between a designer and a computer, generally by the use of a cathode-ray tube (CRT) display and a light pen.

computer art Art form produced by computing equipment.

computer-assisted instruction (CAI) The use of the computer to augment the individual instruction process by providing the student with programmed sequences of instruction under computer control. The manner of sequencing and progressing through the materials permits students to progress at their own rate. CAI is responsive to the individual needs of the individual student. See *authors, COURSEWRITER, PLATO,* and *TICCIT.*

computer-aided instruction See *computer-augmented learning.*

computer-augmented learning (CAL) A method of using a computer system to augment, or supplement, a more conventional instructional system. A typical example would be using simulation programs to aid in the problem solving process in a course of instruction.

computer-based learning (CBL) A term used to embrace all the present forms of educational computing.

computer center See *data processing center.*

computer classifications The two major classifications of computers are digital and analog. A third classification, called hybrid is a combination of both digital and analog computers.

computer code A machine code for a specific computer.

computer control console See *console.*

computer control panel See *control panel.*

computer graphics The use of a computer for drawing lines.

computer family See *family of computers.*

computer instruction See *instruction.*

computer interface unit A device used to connect peripheral devices to a computer. Abbreviated CIU.

computer kit A small, low cost (several hundred dollars) microcomputer in kit form. The user who purchases a computer kit is expected to "build" the microcomputer as he/she would "build" a model airplane or other model. See *home computer, microcomputer,* and *personal computer.*

Computerized checkout systems are used to speed grocery shopping and selling. As grocery items pass over the reading slot, the optical scanning mechanism reads the Universal Product Code data from a symbol affixed to the bottom of each product. This code is transmitted to a computer. The computer looks up the product code, matches the code with the latest price for that product, computes taxes, and sends this information to the cash register terminal. The cash register then visually displays the product name and price and prints a customer receipt.

computer language See *programming language.*

computer-managed instruction (CMI) An application of computers to instruction in which the computer is used as a record keeper, manager and/or prescriber of instruction.

computer network A complex consisting of two or more interconnected computers.

computer operator A person skilled in the operation of the computer and associated peripheral devices. A computer operator also performs other operational functions that are required in a computer center, such as, loading a disk drive, placing cards in the card reader, removing printouts from the line printer rack, and so forth.

computer output microfilm See *computer output microfilm recorder.*

computer output microfilm (COM) recorder A device that records computer output on photosensitive film in microscopic form; the data must be read through a COM reader.

computer program See *program.*

computer programmer A person skilled in the preparation of programs for a computer. A programmer designs, codes, debugs, and documents computer programs. Also called *programmer.* See *coder.*

computer science The field of knowledge embracing all aspects of the design and use of computers.

computer security Involves the protection of computer system equipment and data from unauthorized access.

computer store A new kind of store where you can select, off the shelf, a full computer system or just a few accessories. These stores typically sell software, books, supplies, and periodicals. In a complete computer store, one can examine and operate several types of microcomputer systems.

computer system The physical equipment and instructions; i.e., hardware and software, used as a unit to process data. It includes the central processing unit (CPU), its operating system, and peripheral equipment and programs under its control.

computer utility A service that provides computational ability. A time-shared computer system. Programs as well as data may be made available to the user. The user also may have his own programs immediately available in the central processing unit, may have them on call at the computer utility, or he may load them by transmitting them to the computer prior to using them. Certain data and programs are shared by all users of the service; other data and programs because of proprietary nature, have restricted access. Computer utilities are generally accessed by means of data communication subsystems. See *service bureau.*

computer word A fixed sequence of bits, bytes, or characters treated as a unit and capable of being stored in one storage location. See *word.*

computerized game playing Computers (micro-computers, minicomputers, and larger machines) have been programmed to play a wide variety of games: tic-tac-toe, chess, checkers, go, football, etc. TV games, such as ping-pong are available on many personal computers. Probably the most popular type of personal computer TV game is generally termed "Space War", based on the TV show Star Trek.

Computer-controlled flight simulators are used to train pilots to fly—without ever leaving the ground. The simulator is an exact replica of the cockpit of the jetliner. The turbulence, ground motion, and runway "feel" are provided by the simulator's hydraulic jacks. The runway, vehicular traffic, smoke, and ground lights are creations on a display screen. Everything is tied together by a computer.

computing The act of using computing equipment for processing data.

computing system See *computer system*.

concatenate To link together or join two or more character strings into a single character string.

concatenated data set A collection of logically connected data sets.

concordance An alphabetic list of words and phrases appearing in a document, with an indication of the place those words and phrases appear.

53

concurrent processing The performance of two or more data processing tasks within a specified interval. Contrast with *simultaneous processing.*

condition (1) A given set of circumstances. (2) A definite state of being.

conditional branching See *conditional transfer.*

conditional transfer An instruction that may cause a departure from the sequence of instructions being followed depending upon the result of an operation, the contents of a register, or the settings of an indicator. Contrast with *unconditional transfer.*

conditional statement A statement which is executed only when a certain condition within the routine has been met.

conditioning The improvement of the data transmission properties of a voiceband transmission line by correction of the amplitude and phase characteristics of the line amplifiers.

configuration An assembly of machines, devices, or systems that work together.

configuration management The task of accounting for, controlling, and reporting the planned and actual design of a product throughout its production and operational life.

connect time In time sharing, the length of time you are "on" the computer; that is, the duration of the telephone connection.

connector symbol A flowcharting symbol used to represent a junction in a line of flow, connects broken paths in the line of flow, and connects several pages of the same flowchart. A small circle containing some identifier is used to represent this symbol.

consecutive Pertaining to the occurrence of two sequential events without the intervention of any other such event.

consistency check A routine that ensures that specific input data fall within a predetermined set of criteria.

console The part of a computer system that enables human operators to communicate with a computer.

console operator Same as *computer operator.*

console printer See *console typewriter.*

console typewriter A typewriter on-line to the computer which allows communication between the machine and the *computer operator.*

constant A value that does not change during the execution of the program.

constraints A system of simultaneous mathematical relations which limit the solutions to a problem. Boundaries.

content-addressable memory Same as *associative memory.*

contention A condition on a multipoint communication channel when two or more locations try to transmit at the same time.

contents directory A series of queues that indicate the routines in a given region of internal storage.

contiguous Adjacent or adjoining.

continuous processing The input of transactions into a system in the order they occur, and as soon after they occur as possible.

continuation card A punched card which contains information that was started on a previous punched card.

contour analysis A technique in optical character recognition that uses a spot of light to search for the outline of the character by moving around its exterior edges.

control The function of performing required operations when certain specific conditions occur or interpreting and acting upon instructions. See *control unit.*

control block A storage area through which a particular type of information required for control of the operating system is communicated among its parts.

control cards Punched cards that contain input data required for a specific application of a general routine such as a generator or operating system; e.g., one of a series of cards that directs an operating system to load and initiate execution of a particular program.

control circuits The electrical circuits within a computer which interpret the program instructions and cause the appropriate operations to be performed.

control clerk A person having responsibility for performing duties associated with the control over data processing operations.

control console That part of a computer system used for communication between the console operator or service engineer and the computer.

control data One or more items of data used as control to identify, select, execute, or modify another routine, record, file, operation, or data value.

control panel (1) A part of a computer control console that contains manual controls. (2) A hand-wired plugboard used to control the operations of unit record devices. See *console* and *plugboard*.

control program An operating system program responsible for the overall management of the computer and its resources. See *operating system*.

control punch A specific code punched in a card to cause the machine to perform a specific operation.

control section The part of the central processing unit responsible for directing the operation of the computer in accordance with the instructions in the program. Same as *control unit*.

control sequence The normal order of selection of instructions by a digital computer wherein it follows one instruction order at a time.

control statement An operation that terminates the sequential execution of instructions by transferring control to a statement elsewhere in the program.

control unit The portion of the central processing unit that directs the step-by-step operation of the entire computing system. Same as *control section*.

conversational mode A mode of operation that implies a "dialog" between a computer and its user, in which the computer program examines the input supplied by the user and formulates questions or comments which are directed back and to the user. See *interactive processing* and *logging-in*.

conversational system See *interactive system*.

conversion (1) The process of changing information from one form of representation to another; such as, from the language of one type of computer to that of another or from punch cards to magnetic disk. (2) The process of changing from one data processing method to another, or from one type of equipment to another. (3) The process of changing a number written in one base to the base of another numeral system.

conversion table A table comparing numerals in two different numeral systems.

converter (1) A device which converts information recorded on one medium to another medium; e.g., a unit which accepts information from punched cards and records the information on magnetic disks. (2) A device that converts information in one form into information in another form; e.g., analog to digital.

coordinate indexing A system of indexing individual documents by descriptors of equal rank, so that a library can be searched for a combination of one or more descriptors; an indexing technique where the interrelations of terms are shown by coupling individual words.

copy To reproduce data in a new location or other destination, leaving the source data unchanged, although the physical form of the result may differ from that of the source. For example, a copy of a deck of cards onto a magnetic disk. Contrast with *duplicate*.

core See *magnetic core*.

core plane See *magnetic core plane*.

core storage A form of storage device utilizing magnetic cores. See *magnetic core storage*.

corner cut A diagonal cut at the corner of a punch card. It is used as a means of identifying groups of related cards.

corrective maintenance The activity of detecting, isolating and correcting failures after occurrence. See *preventive maintenance*.

counter A device (e.g., a register or computer storage location) used to represent the number of occurrences of an event.

coupling An interaction between systems or between properties of a system.

COURSEWRITER A programming language used to write instructional programs for computer assisted instruction (CAI) systems.

cpi An abbreviation for characters per inch.

CPM An acronym for *Critical Path Method*.

cps An abbreviation for characters per second.

CPS An acronym for Conversation Programming System. Refers generally to a computer system in which input and output are handled by a remote terminal and employing time sharing so that the user obtains what appears to be an immediate response. Used more specifically as CPS-PL/I to mean an IBM devised subset of the PL/I programming language used with remote terminals.

CPU An acronym for *Central Processing Unit.*

CR An acronym for *Carriage Return.*

CRAM An acronym for Card Random Access Method. An auxiliary storage device that uses removable magnetic cards each of which is capable of storing data in magnetic form. The storage unit is manufactured by NCR Corporation.

critical path The path through the network that defines the shortest possible time in which the entire project can be completed. See *critical path method* and *PERT.*

critical path method A management technique for control of large-scale long-term projects, involving analysis and determination of each critical step necessary for project completion. Abbreviated CPM. See *PERT.*

CROM An acronym for Control ROM, an integral part of most central processing unit (CPU) chips. The CROM is the storage for the microinstructions which the CPU assembles into a sequence to form complex "macroinstructions", such as Multiply or Branch-On-Negative Accumulator which the computer user normally uses.

cross assembler Refers to an assembler run on one computer for the purpose of translating instructions for a different computer.

cross compiling/assembling A technique where one uses a minicomputer, large scale computer, or time-sharing service to write and debug programs for subsequent use on microcomputers.

cross reference dictionary A printed listing that identifies all references of an assembled program to a specific label. In many systems this listing is provided immediately after a source program has been assembled.

crosscheck To check the computing by two different methods.

crosstalk The unwanted energy transferred from one

circuit, called the "disturbing" circuit, to another circuit, called the "disturbed" circuit.

CRT An acronym for *Cathode Ray Tube.*

cryogenics The study and use of devices which utilize the properties assumed by materials at temperatures near absolute zero.

cue Same as *call.*

cursor A moving, sliding, or blinking symbol on a CRT, which indicates where the next character will appear.

cybernetics The branch of learning which seeks to integrate the theories and studies of communication and control in machines and living organisms. See *Norbert Wiener.*

cycle As related to computer storage — a periodic sequence of events occurring when information is transferred to or from the storage device of a computer. It is the time it takes to reference an address, remove the data, and be ready to select it again.

cycle time The minimum time interval between the starts of successive accesses to a storage location.

cyclic code Same as *gray code.*

cyclic shift A shift in which the digits dropped off at one end of a word are returned at the other in a circular fashion; for example, if register holds eight digits, 23456789, the result of the cyclic shift two columns to the left would be to change the contents of the register to 45678923.

cylinder As related to magnetic disks, a vertical column of tracks on a magnetic disk file unit.

D

DASD Acronym for Direct Access Storage Device. A device such as a magnetic disk storage unit or a magnetic drum storage unit.

data A formalized representation of facts or concepts suitable for communication, interpretation, or processing by people or by automatic means.

data administrator Person in charge of the data base and its use.

data bank See *data base.*

data base A data base is the collection of all data used and produced by a computer program. In large systems, data base analysis is usually concerned with large quantities of data stored in disk and tape files. Smaller personal computer systems are more frequently concerned with data base allocations of available memory locations between program and data storage areas.

data base administrator A person who is responsible for the creation of the information system data base and once it is established, for maintaining its security, and developing procedures for recovery from disaster.

data base management A systematic approach to storing, updating and retrieval of information stored as data items, usually in the form of records in a file, where many users, or even many remote installations, will use common data banks.

data base management system A software system for managing the storage, access, updating, and maintenance of a data base.

data bus A bus system which interconnects the CPU, storage, and all the input/output devices of a computer system, for the purpose of exchanging data.

data byte The 8-bit binary number that the microprocessor will use in an arithmetic or logical operation or store in memory.

data capturing Gathering or collecting information for computer handling; first step in job processing. Also called *data collection.*

data cell A magnetic storage device developed by the IBM Corporation. A direct access device that handles data recorded on magnetic strips arranged in cells.

data collection (1) The gathering of source data to be entered into a data processing system. (2) The act of bringing data from one or more points to a central point. Also called *data capturing.*

data communications The movement of encoded information by means of electrical transmission systems.

data conversion The process of changing the form of data representation — for example, punched card to magnetic disks.

data editing A procedure to check for irregularities in input data. See *edit.*

data item An item of data, used to represent a single value.

data link Equipment which permits the transmission of information in data format. See *channel.*

data management A general term that collectively describes those functions of a system that provide access to hardware, enforce data storage conventions, and regulate the use of input/output devices.

data manipulation language A language for manipulating data in a data base.

data medium The material in or on which a specific physical variable may represent data, e.g., magnetic disk, paper tape, or punched cards.

data name The name of the variable used to indicate a data value; e.g., PI for 3.14159.

data origination The translation of information from its original form into machine-sensible form.

Data Phone The name applied by AT & T to the members of a family of devices used for providing data communications over telephone facilities. See *data set.*

data preparation The process of organizing information and storing it in a form that can be input to the computer.

data processing (1) One or more operations performed on data to achieve a desired objective. (2) The functions of a computer center. (3) A term used in reference to operations performed by data processing equipment.

data processing center A computer center equipped with devices capable of receiving information, processing it according to human-made instructions, and producing the computed results.

data processing manager The person who runs the information processing center which usually includes the operation of the computer. The biggest part of his job is concerned with developing new systems, and then keeping them running.

data processing system A network of data processing hardware and software capable of accepting information, processing it according to a plan, and producing the desired results.

data processor Any device capable of performing operations on data, e.g., a desk calculator or a digital computer.

data reduction The process of transforming raw data into useful, condensed, or simplified intelligence. Often adjusting, scaling, smoothing, compacting, editing, and ordering operations are used in the process.

data security Involves the protection of data from unauthorized access. See *computer security, disk library* and *tape library.*

data set A device which permits the transmission of data over communication lines by changing the form of the data at one end so that it can be carried over the lines; another data set at the other end changes the data back to its original form so that it is acceptable to the machine (computer, etc.) at that end. The *Data Phone* is an example. Same as *modem.*

data sheet A special form used to record input values in a format convenient for keypunching. See *coding form.*

data storage devices Units for storing large quantities (millions) of characters. Typically magnetic disk units, magnetic tape units, magnetic drums, and magnetic card units.

data structure The relationship between data items.

data transmission The sending of data from one part of a system to another part. See *data communications.*

DATAPHONE A trade mark of the AT & T Company to identify the data sets manufactured and supplied by the Bell

System for use in the transmission of data over the telephone network.

datum A unit of information; e.g., a computer word.

DDL An acronym for Data Description Language. A language for declaring data structures in a data base.

deblocking Extracting a logical record from a block or group of logical records.

debug To detect, locate, and remove all mistakes in a computer program and any malfunctions in the computing system itself. See *bug, debugging aids,* and *test data.*

debugging aids Computer routines that are helpful in debugging programs; e.g., trace, snapshot dump, or post mortem dump.

deceleration time The time required to stop a magnetic tape after reading or recording the last piece of data from a record on that tape.

decimal code Describing a form of notation by which each decimal digit separately is expressed in some other number system.

decimal digit A numeral in the decimal numeral system. The radix of the decimal system is 10 and the following symbols are used: 0, 1, 2, 3, 4, 5, 6, 7, 8, and 9.

decimal number A numeral, usually of more than one digit, representing a sum, in which the quantity represented by each digit is based on the radix of ten.

decimal system Base-10 positional notation system.

decimal-to-binary conversion The process of converting a numeral written to the base ten to the equivalent numeral written to the base two.

decimal-to-hexadecimal conversion The process of converting a numeral written to the base ten to the equivalent numeral written to the base sixteen.

decimal-to-octal conversion The process of converting a numeral written to the base 10 to the equivalent numeral written to the base eight.

decision The computer operation of determining if a certain relationship exists between words in storage or registers and taking alternative courses of action.

decision instruction An instruction that effects the

selection of a branch of a program; e.g., a conditional jump instruction.

decision symbol A flowcharting symbol used to indicate a choice or branching in the information processing path. A diamond shaped figure is used to represent this symbol.

decision table A table listing all the contigencies to be considered in the description of a problem, together with the corresponding actions to be taken. Decision tables are sometimes used instead of flowcharts to describe the operations of a program.

decision tree A pictorial representation of the alternatives in any situation.

declaration statement A part of a computer program that defines the nature of other elements of the program or reserves parts of the hardware for special use.

decode Translate or determine the meaning of coded information. Contrast with *encode.*

decoder (1) A device that decodes. (2) A matrix of switching elements that selects one or more output channels according to the combination of input signals present.

decollate To separate the plies of a multipart form or paper stock.

decrement Decreasing the value of a quantity.

dedicated computer A computer whose use is reserved for a particular task.

default option An assumption made by a system or language translator when no specific choice is given by the user or his program.

deferred entry An entry into a subroutine that occurs as a result of a deferred exit from the program that passed control to it.

deferred exit The passing of control to a subroutine at a time determined by an asynchronous event rather than at a predictable time.

definition of a problem The art of compiling logic in the form of algorithms, flowcharts, and program descriptions which clearly explain and define the problem.

degausser A device that is used to erase information from a magnetic device, i.e., magnetic tape.

64

delay The amount of time by which an event is retarded.

deletion record A new record which will replace or remove an existing record of a master file.

delay line storage A storage device that consists of a delay line and means for regenerating and reinserting information into the delay line; used in early computers.

delete To remove or eliminate.

delimit To fix the limits of — for example, to establish maximum and minimum limits of a specific variable.

delimiter A special character, often a comma or space, used to separate variable names or items in a list, or to separate one string of characters from another, as in the separation of data items.

demodulation In data communications, the process of retrieving an original signal from a modulated carrier wave. This technique is used in data sets to make communication signals compatible with computer terminal signals.

demodulator A device that receives signals transmitted over a communications link and converts them into electrical pulses, or bits, that can serve as inputs to a data processing machine. Contrast with *modulator*.

denominator In the expression A/B, B is the denominator and A is the numerator.

dense binary code A code in which all possible states of the binary pattern are used.

descending sort A sort in which the final sequence of records is such that the successive keys compare "less than" or "equal to."

descriptor A significant word which helps to categorize or index information. Sometimes called a *keyword*.

design automation The use of computers in the design and production of circuit packages, new computers, and other electronic equipment.

desk checking A manual checking process in which representative sample data items, used for detecting errors in program logic, are traced through the program before the latter is executed on the computer.

destructive read The process of destroying the information in a location by reading the contents.

detail file A file containing relatively transient

65

information; for example, records of individual transactions that occurred during a particular period of time. Synonymous with *transaction file*. Contrast with *master file*.

detail printing An operation where a line of printing occurs for each card read by an accounting machine.

deterministic model A mathematical model for the study of data of known fixed values and direct cause-and-effect relationships.

device A mechanical or electrical unit with a specific purpose.

device code The 8-bit code for a specific input or output device.

device independence The ability to command input/output operations without regard to the characteristics of the input/output devices.

device name The general name for a kind of device; e.g., model 3330 disk or 2240 CPU.

diagnosis The process of isolating malfunctions in computing equipment and detecting mistakes in programs and systems.

diagnostic routine A routine designed to locate a malfunction in the central processing unit or a peripheral device.

diagnostics Messages to the user automatically printed by a computer which pinpoint improper commands and errors in logic. Sometimes called *error messages*.

diagram A schematic representation of a sequence of operations or routines. See *flowchart*.

dial-up In data communications, the use of a dial or push-button telephone to initiate a station-to-station telephone call.

dichotomizing search See *binary search*.

dictionary (1) Words arranged alphabetically and usually defined. (2) A lexicon in alphabetic order.

die The tiny rectangular pieces of a circular wafer of semiconductor silicon, sawed or sliced during the fabrication of integrated circuits or transistors.

difference engine A machine designed by Charles Babbage in 1822 which mechanized a calculating function called the "method of differences." The machine was never built, however, because of inadequate engineering capabilities.

differential analyzer A machine built in 1930 which was able to calculate differential equations. It was entirely mechanical, having no electrical parts.

digit One of the symbols of a numbering system that is used to designate a quantity.

digit place In positional notation, the site where a symbol such as a digit is located in a word representing a numeral.

digit punching position The area on a punch card reserved to represent a decimal digit; i.e., a punch in rows 1, 2, . . . , 9.

digital Pertaining to data in the form of digits. Contrast with *analog.*

digital computer A device that manipulates digital data and performs arithmetic and logic operations on these data. See *computer.*

digital data Data represented in discrete, discontinuous form, as contrsted with analog data represented in continuous form.

digital plotter See *plotter.*

digital sorting A sort which uses a technique similar to sorting on tabulation machines. The elapsed time is directly proportional to the number of characters in the sequencing key and the volume of data. Also called *radix sorting.*

digital-to-analog converter Mechanical or electronic devices used to convert discrete digital numbers to continuous analog signals. Abbreviated D-A converter. Opposite of *analog-to-digital converter.*

digitize To convert a measurement into a digital value. In computing, this is normally done automatically and consists of converting an electrical signal into a binary number. See *analog-to-digital converter.*

dimension The maximum size or the number and arrangement of the elements of an array.

diode An electronic device used to permit current flow in one direction and to inhibit current flow in the opposite direction.

DIP An acronym for Dual In-line Package. A logic device on which a chip is mounted.

direct access Pertaining to the process of obtaining data from or placing data into storage where the time required for such access is independent of the location of the data most recently obtained or placed in storage. Also called *random access*. Contrast with *serial access*.

direct address An address that specifies the storage location of an operand. Contrast with *indirect address*.

disc Alternate spelling for disk. See *magnetic disk storage*.

discrete Pertaining to distinct elements or to representation by means of distinct elements such as characters.

disk See *floppy disk* and *magnetic disk*.

disk library A special room which houses a file of disk packs under secure, environmentally-controlled conditions.

disk pack A set of detachable magnetic disks. Example: A disk pack might consist of eleven disks, 35.56 cm (14 inches) in diameter, mounted on a central spindle. The pack would weigh about 4.536 kgs (10 pounds) and hold some 29 million characters of data.

disk storage See *magnetic disk storage*.

diskette A floppy disk. A low cost bulk storage medium for microcomputers and minicomputers.

dispatching priority A number assigned to tasks, and used to determine precedence for use of the central processing unit in a multitask situation.

dispersed data processing Same as *distributed data processing*.

displacement The difference between the base address and the actual machine language address.

display A visual representation of data.

display unit A device which provides a visual representation of data. See *cathode ray tube* and *plasma display*.

distributed data processing A concept where a company supplements its main computer system (often called the home office computer) with field office terminals. The field office terminals can be used to do local data processing operations without tying down the home office computer. Limited data communications can occur between the home office computer and the field office terminals, thus providing for a company wide communication system. Contrast with *centralized data processing.*

dividend In the division operation A/B; A is the dividend and B is the divisor. The result is the quotient and remainder.

divisor The quantity which is used to divide another quantity.

DMA An acronym for Direct Memory Access. A method by which data can be transferred between peripheral devices and internal memory without intervention by the central processing unit.

DNC An acronym for Direct Numerical Control. Computer control of automatic machine tools. Control is applied at discrete points in the process, rather than continuously applied. See *APT* and *numerical control.*

document retrieval Acquiring data from storage devices and, possibly, manipulating the data and subsequently preparing a report.

documentation The preparation of documents, during systems analysis and subsequent programming, that describe such things as the system, the programs prepared, and the changes made at later dates.

documentor A program designed to use data processing methods in the production and maintenance of program flowcharts, text material, and other types of tabular or graphic information.

doping The process of introducing impurity elements into the crystalline structure of pure silicon during semiconductor fabrication.

DOS An acronym for Disk Operating System.

double-dabble Process of converting binary numbers into their decimal equivalents.

double precision Pertaining to the use of two computer words to represent a number in order to gain increased precision.

double punch More than one numeric punch in any one column of a card.

downtime The length of time a computer system is inoperative due to a malfunction.

DPMA An acronym for Data Processing Management Association. A professional data processing organization whose primary purpose is to develop and promote business methods and education in data processing and data processing management.

DPMA certificate A certificate given by the Data Processing Management Association which indicates that a person has a certain level of competence in the field of data processing. The certificate is obtained by passing an examination that is offered yearly.

drain One of the three connecting terminals of a Field Effect Transistor, the other two being the *source* and the *gate*. If the charge carriers are positive, the conventional current flows from the source to the drain.

driver A software driver is a series of instructions the computer follows to reformat data for transfer to and from a particular peripheral device. The electrical and mechanical requirements are different from one kind of device to another and the software drivers are used to standardize the format of data between them and the central processor.

drop out In data transmission, a momentary loss in signal, usually due to the effect of noise or system malfunction.

drum See *magnetic drum*.

drum printer A printing device which uses a drum embossed with alphabetic and numeric characters. A type of *line printer*.

drum sorting A sort program that utilizes magnetic drums for auxiliary storage during sorting.

drum storage See *magnetic drum storage*.

dummy argument Variables, used as function arguments, that do not have any values.

dummy instruction (1) An artificial instruction or address inserted in a list to serve a purpose other than the execution as an instruction. (2) An instruction in a routine that, in itself, does not perform any functions. Often used to provide a point in which to terminate a program loop.

dump The data that results from a "dumping" process. See *post mortem dump* and *snapshot dump*.

dumping Copying all or part of the contents of a storage unit, usually from the computer's internal storage into an auxiliary storage unit or onto a line printer. See *dump, post morten dump,* and *snapshot dump.*

duplex Relates to a communications system or equipment capable of transmission in both directions. See *full duplex* and *half duplex.*

duplex channel A channel which allows simultaneous transmission in both directions. See *full duplex, half duplex* and *simplex.*

duplexing The use of duplicate computers, peripheral equipment, circuitry, so that in the event of a component failure an alternate component can enable the system to continue.

duplicate To copy so that the result remains in the same physical form as the source; e.g., to make a new punch card with the same pattern of holes as an original punch card. Contrast with *copy.*

duplication check A check requiring that the results of two independent performances of the same operation be identical. The check may be made concurrently on duplicate equipment or at a later time on the same equipment.

dyadic operation An operation on two operands.

dynamic dump A dump taken during the execution of a program.

dynamic relocation The movement of part or all of an active (i.e., currently operating) program from one region of storage to another, with all necessary address references being adjusted to enable proper execution of the program to continue in its new location.

dynamic scheduling Job scheduling that is determined by the computer on a moment-to-moment basis, depending upon the circumstances.

dynamic storage A memory device which must be constantly recharged or "refreshed" at frequent intervals to avoid loss of data. A very volatile memory.

dynamic storage allocation Automatic storage allocation. See *storage allocation.*

E

EAM An acronym for *Electronic Accounting Machine.* Usually refers to unit record equipment.

EAROM An acronym for Electrically Alternable ROM. See *EPROM.*

EBCDIC An acronym for Extended Binary Coded Decimal Interchange Code. An 8-bit code used to represent data in modern computers. EBCDIC can represent up to 256 distinct characters and is the principal code used in many of the current computers.

echo check A check upon the accuracy of a data transfer operation in which the data received is transmitted back to the source and compared with the original data.

Eckert, J. Presper Co-inventor of the ENIAC, an early electronic computer.

ECL An acronym for Emitter Coupled Logic, also called Current Mode Logic. ECL is faster than TTL, but much less popular.

edge-punched card A card into which data may be recorded by punching holes along one edge in a pattern similar to that used for punched tape. Hole positions are arranged to form coded patterns in five, six, seven, or eight channels and usually represent data in a binary code decimal system.

edit (1) To check the correctness of data. (2) To change as necessary the form of data, adding or deleting certain characters. For example, part of program can edit data for printing, adding special symbols, spacing, deleting nonsignificant zeros, etc.

editing See *data editing.*

EDP An acronym for *Electronic Data Processing.* Data processing performed largely by electronic digital computers.

EDSAC An acronym for Electronic Delayed Storage Automatic Computer. The first digital computer to feature the stored program concept. It was developed in Great Britain in 1949 at Cambridge University.

EDVAC An acronym for Electronic Discrete Variable Automatic Computer. Developed at the Moore School of Electrical Engineering, University of Pennsylvania in 1949. It was the first U.S. built computer that featured a stored program unit.

effective address The address that is derived by performing any specified address modification operations upon a specified address.

EFTS An acronym for Electronic Funds Transfer System. A system for transferring funds from one account to another with electronic equipment rather than with paper media such as checks.

electronic accounting machine Pertaining to data processing equipment that is predominantly electromechanical; e.g., keypunch, mechanical sorter, tabulator, or collator.

electromagnetic delay line A delay line whose operation is based on the time of propagation of electromagnetic waves through distributed or lumped capacitance and inductance. Used in early computers.

electromechanical A system for processing data that uses both electrical and mechanical principles.

electronic data processing Data processing performed largely by electronic equipment.

electronic data processing system The general term used to define a system for data processing by means of machines utilizing electronic circuitry at electronic speed, as opposed to electromechanical equipment.

electronically programmable Pertains to a Programmable ROM (Read Only Memory) or any other digital device in which the data 1's and 0's in binary code can be entered electrically, usually by the user with a piece of equipment called a *PROM Programmer.*

electronics The branch of physics concerned primarily with the natural and controlled flow of electrons through various substances.

electrostatic printer A high-speed line printer. Report page images are magnetized on paper, and then the magnetized paper is passed through an ink fog. The ink adheres to the magnetized spots. Later, the ink is baked into the paper producing the final output sheets.

element An item of data within an array.

elements of a microcomputer Microprocessor for the central processing unit, program memory (usually ROM), data storage (usually RAM), and input/output circuitry, and clock generators.

MICROPROCESSOR
(CPU)

PROGRAM STORAGE
(usually ROM, PROM, or EPROM)

PROGRAM AND DATA STORAGE
(usually RAM)

INPUT/OUTPUT CIRCUITRY

PERIPHERAL SUPPORT CHIPS
(clock)

Major components of a microcomputer.

eleven-punch A punch in the second row from the top of a Hollerith punched card. Synonymous with *X-punch*.

emulate To imitate one system with another, such that the imitating system accepts the same data, executes the same programs and achieves the same results as the imitated system.

emulator A type of program or device that allows user programs, written for one kind of computer system, to be run on another system.

encode To translate information into a code. Contrast with *decode*.

end-around carry A carry from the most significant digit place to the least significant digit place.

end-around shift See *circular shift*.

end mark A code or signal which indicates termination of a unit of data.

end-of-file Termination or point of completion of a quantity of data. End of file marks are used to indicate this point on magnetic files. Abbreviated EOF. See *end-of-tape marker*.

end-of-message Termination of a message. Abbreviated EOM.

end-of-tape marker A marker on a magnetic tape used to indicate the end of the permissible recording area.

engineering units Units of measure as applied to a process variable; e.g., PSI, Degrees C., etc.

ENIAC An acronym for Electronic Numerical Integrator And Calculator. An early all-electronic digital computer. It was built by J. Mauchly and J. Eckert at the Moore School of Electrical Engineering, University of Pennsylvania in 1946.

entry point Any location in a routine to which control can be passed by another routine.

EOF An acronym for *End-of-File*. When all the records in a file have been processed, the computer is said to have encountered an "end-of-file" condition.

EOJ An acronym for End-of-Job.

EOM An acronym for End of Message. Termination of a message.

75

EPROM An acronym for Erasable PROM. One of the latest types of monolithic memory. It can be programmed in the field by the user, and it can also be erased and reprogrammed with different information. Once it has been programmed the EPROM memory acts just the same as ROM. This is a memory that cannot be written into, but it can be read as many times as necessary. The EPROM will be the program memory most frequently used by experimenters, hobbyists, etc. and others who must make frequent changes to their programs. They can do it themselves if they have the proper equipment - a *PROM Programmer*. See *PROM* and *ROM*.

equality The idea expressed by the equal sign, written =.

equation A mathematical sentence with an = sign between two expressions which name the same number; e.g., a+b = b+a is an equation.

equipment Part of a computer system. See *computer, hardware* and *peripheral equipment*.

erasable storage A storage medium which can be erased and reused. Magnetic disk, drum, or tape are mediums that can be erased and reused while punched cards or punched paper tape cannot.

erase To remove data from storage without replacing it.

EROM An acronym for Erasable ROM. An *EPROM*.

error The general term referring to any deviation of a computed or a measured quantity from the theoretically correct or true value. Contrast with *fault, malfunction* and *mistake*. See *intermittent error,* and *round-off error*.

error analysis The branch of numerical analysis concerned with studying the error aspects of numerical analysis procedures. It includes the study of errors that arise in a computation because of the pecularities of computer arithmetic.

error-correcting code (1) A code in which each acceptable expression conforms to specific rules of construction. Nonacceptable expressions are also defined. If certain types of errors occur in an acceptable expression, an equivalent will result and the error can be corrected. (2) A code in which the forbidden pulse combination produced by the gain or loss of a bit will indicate which bit is wrong. Same as *self-correcting code*.

error correction A system that detects and inherently provides correction for errors caused by transmission equipment or facilities.

error-detection code (1) A code in which each expression conforms to specific rules of construction. When expressions occur that do not conform to the rules of these constructions, an error is indicated. (2) A code in which errors produce forbidden combinations. A single error-detecting code produces a forbidden combination if a digit gains or loses a single bit. A double error-detecting code produces a forbidden combination if a digit gains or loses either one or two bits, etc. Also called a *self-checking code*.

error file A file generated during data processing to retain erroneous information sensed by the computer, often printed out as an error report.

error message A printed statement indicating the computer has detected a mistake or malfunction.

error rate In data communications, a measure of quality of circuit or equipment; the number of erroneous bits or characters in a sample.

error ratio The ratio of the number of data units in error to the total number of data units.

evaluate To find the value of.

event An occurrence or happening.

excess-three code A binary coded decimal notation in which each decimal digit X is represented by the binary numeral of X plus three.

exchange buffering A technique using data chaining for eliminating the need to move data in internal storage.

exchangeable disk See *disk pack*.

exclusive OR The Boolean operator which gives a truth table value of true if only one of the two variables it connects is true. If both variables it connects are true, this value is false.

executable A program statement that gives an instruction of some computational operation to be performed then; e.g., assignment statements are executable. Contrast with *nonexecutable*.

execution Performance of the instructions given by a program. Same as *run*.

77

execution time See *run time.*

execute cycle The period of time during which a machine instruction is interpreted and the indicated operation is performed on the specified operand.

executive A master program that controls the execution of other programs. Often used synonymously with *monitor, supervisory system,* and *operating system.*

expansion card A card added to a system for the purpose of mounting additional chips or circuits to expand the system capability.

exponent A symbol or number written above and to the right of another symbol or number that denotes the number of times the latter is used as a factor.

exponentiation The mathematical process of raising a number to a power of a base; e.g., 2^4.

exponential smoothing A forecasting technique.

expression A source language combination of one or more operations.

external data file Data that is stored separately from the program that processes it.

external label An identification label attached to the outside of a file medium holder identifying the file; e.g., a paper label or sticker attached to the cover containing a magnetic disk pack.

external references A reference to a symbol defined in another routine.

external sort The second phase of a multipass sort program, wherein strings of data are continually merged until one string of sequenced data is formed.

external storage See *auxiliary storage.*

external symbol A control section name, entry point name, or external reference; a symbol contained in the external symbol dictionary.

external symbol dictionary Control information associated with an object program which identifies the external symbols in the program.

extract To remove specific information from a computer word as determined by a mask or filter.

F

fabricated language Same as *symbolic language.*

facilities management The use of an independent service organization to operate and manage a data processing installation.

facsimile (1) Transmission of pictures, maps, diagrams, etc. The image is scanned at the transmitter, reconstructed at the receiving station, and duplicated on some form of paper. (2) A precise reproduction of an original document; an exact copy. (3) A hard-copy reproduction. Abbreviated FAX.

factor analysis A mathematical technique for studying the interaction of many factors to determine the most significant factors and the degree of significance.

fail-soft system A system which continues to process data despite the failure of parts of the system. Usually accompanied by a deterioration in performance.

failure prediction A technique which attempts to determine the failure schedule of specific parts or equipments so that they may be discarded and replaced before failure occurs.

family of computers Series of central processing units allegedly of the same logical design, but of different speeds. This philosophy is supposed to enable the user to start with a slower/less expensive CPU and grow to a faster/more expensive one as the work load builds up, without having to change the rest of the computer system.

FAMOS An acronym for Floating gate Avalanche injection MOS, a fabrication technology for charge storage devices such as PROMs.

fan-in The number of signal inputs to a digital logic element.

fan-out The number of TTL unit loads a given TTL device output can supply or drive, under worst case conditions.

father file When a file update program is run, the old master file is termed the "father file." The updated file is termed the "son file." The file that was used to create the father file is termed the "grandfather file."

fault A condition that causes a component, a computer, or a peripheral device to not perform to its design specifications; e.g., a broken wire or a short circuit. Contrast with *error, malfunction* and *mistake*.

FAX See *facsimile.*

feasibility study Concerned with a definition of the data processing problem, together with alternative solutions, a recommended course of action, and a working plan for designing and installing the system.

feed holes Holes punched in a paper tape to enable it to be driven by a sprocket wheel.

feedback A means of automatic control in which the actual state of a process is measured and used to obtain a quantity that modifies the input in order to initiate the activity of the control system.

FET An acronym for *Field Effect Transistor.*

fetch To locate and load a quantity of data from storage.

field A group of related characters treated as a unit — e.g., a group of adjacent card columns used to represent an hourly wage rate. An item in a record.

field effect transistor A three terminal semiconductor device which acts as a variable charge storage element. The most commonly used type in microcomputers is the Metallic Oxide Semiconductor (MOS) transistor. Abbreviated FET.

fieldata code The U.S. Military code used in data processing as a compromise between conflicting manufacturers' codes.

FIFO An acronym for First In-First Out.

file A collection of related records treated as a unit.

file conversion Changing the file medium or structure.

file gap See *interblock gap.*

file label A label identifying a file.

file layout The arrangement and structure of data in a file, including the sequence and size of its components.

file maintenance The updating of a file to reflect the effects of nonperiodic changes by adding, altering, or deleting data; e.g., the addition of new programs to a program library on magnetic disks.

file processing The periodic updating of master files to reflect the effects of current data, often transaction data contained in detail files; e.g., a monthly inventory run updating the master inventory file.

file protect ring Used to protect data on magnetic tape. Accidental writing on the tape is prevented by removing the ring from the tape reel.

file storage Devices which can hold a reservoir of mass data within the computer system. Magnetic disk units, magnetic tape units, and magnetic card units are examples of file storage devices.

filter See *mask.*

firmware Software instructions or data that are stored in a fixed or "firm" way, usually implemented in a ROM, PROM, or EPROM, as opposed to software programs stored on paper or magnetic media and which must be entered into the RAM memory of the computer to be used. Changes can often be made by exchanging the memory chip for an alternate unit. Firmware is built into the computer to make its operation simpler for the user to understand.

first generation The first commercially available computers, introduced with UNIVAC I in 1951, and terminated with the development of the transistor in 1959. First generation computers are characterized by their use of vacuum tubes. Now museum pieces.

fixed area That portion of internal storage that has been assigned to specific programs or data areas.

fixed-head disk unit A storage device consisting of one or more magnetically coded disks, on the surface of which data is stored in the form of magnetic spots arranged in a manner to represent binary data. These data are arranged in circular tracks around the disks and are accessible to reading and writing by read-write heads assigned one per track. Data from a given track are read or written sequentially as the disk rotates under the read-write head.

fixed-length record A record that always contains the same number of characters. Contrast with *variable-length record.*

fixed point Pertaining to a number system in which each number is represented by a single set of digits and the position of the radix point is implied by the manner in which the numbers are used. Contrast with *floating point.*

fixed point arithmetic (1) A method of calculation in which operations take place in an invariant manner, and in which the computer does not consider the location of the radix point. This is illustrated by desk calculators with which the operator must keep track of the decimal point. Similarly with many automatic computers, in which the location of the radix point is the computer user's responsibility. (2) A type of arithmetic in which the operands and results of all arithmetic operations must be properly scaled to have a magnitude between certain fixed values.

fixed size records File elements each of which has the same number of words, characters, bytes, bits, fields, etc.

fixed storage Storage whose contents are not alterable by computer instructions; e.g., *read-only storage.* See *ROM* and *PROM.*

fixed word length Pertaining to a machine word or operand that always has the same number of bits, bytes, or characters. Contrast with *variable word length.*

flag (1) An indicator used frequently to tell some later part of a program that some condition occurred earlier. (2) A symbol used to mark a record for special attention. For example, on a listing of a program, all statements which contain errors may be flagged for the attention of the program writer.

flat-bed plotter See *plotter.*

flexowriter A form of typewriter accepting paper tape input. Used as an input/output device with many older computers.

flip-flop A device or circuit containing active elements, capable of assuming either one of two stable states at a given time. Synonymous with *toggle.*

floating point A form of number representation in which quantities are represented by a number called the mantissa multiplied by a power of the number base. Contrast with *fixed point.* See *characteristic* and *mantissa.*

floating point arithmetic A method of calculation which automatically accounts for the location of the radix point.

floating point routine A set of subroutines which cause a computer to execute floating point arithmetic. These routines are used to simulate floating point operations on a computer with no built-in floating point hardware.

floppy disk   A flexible disk (*diskette*) of oxide-coated mylar that is stored in paper or plastic envelopes. The entire envelope is inserted in the disk unit. Floppy disks are a low-cost storage that is used widely with minicomputers and microcomputers. See *magnetic disk.*

flow   A general term to indicate a sequence of events.

flow diagram   See *flowchart.*

flowchart   A diagram that uses symbols and interconnecting lines to show (1) the logic and sequence of specific program operations (program flowchart) or (2) a system of processing to achieve objectives (system flowchart).

flowchart symbol   A symbol used to represent operations, data, flow, or equipment on a flowchart. See *annotation symbol, connector symbol, decision symbol, input/output symbol, processing symbol,* and *terminal symbol.*

flowchart template   A plastic guide containing cutouts of the flowchart symbols that is used in the preparation of a flowchart.

flowchart text   The descriptive information that is associated with flowchart symbols.

flowline   On a flowchart, a line representing a connecting path between flowchart symbols.

FLOW-MATIC   The first automatic programming language. It was developed for the UNIVAC II computer.

font   A group of characters of one size and style; e.g., the type font used in this book is 10-point Chelmsford.

force   To intervene manually in a program and cause the computer to execute a jump instruction.

forecast   A projection of the past into the future.

foreground processing   The automatic execution of the computer programs that have been designed to preempt the use of the computing facilities.

foreground program   A program that has a high priority and therefore takes precedence over other concurrently operating programs in a computer system using multiprogramming techniques. Contrast with *background program.*

form (1) A preprinted document requiring additional information to make it meaningful. (2) The format of the program output.

formal language A system consisting of a well-defined, usually finite, set of characters and rules for combining characters with one another to form words or other expressions but without assignment of permanent meaning to such words or expressions.

formal logic The study of the structure and form of valid argument without regard to the meaning of the terms in the argument.

format The arrangement of data.

formula A rule expressed as an equation; e.g., $C = 2\pi r$ is the formula for finding the circumference of a circle.

FORTRAN An acronym for FORmulaTRANslator. A higher level programming language used to perform mathematical, scientific, and engineering computations. FORTRAN has been approved as an American Standard programming language in two versions (FORTRAN and Basic FORTRAN). A widely used programming language.

four-address instruction A machine instruction usually consisting of the addresses of two operands, the address for storing the result, the address of the next instruction, the command to be executed, and miscellaneous indices.

FPLA An acronym for Field Programmable Logic Array. A FPLA can be programmed by the user in the field, whereas an ordinary PLA is programmable only by masking at the semiconductor manufacturer's factory.

frame An area, one recording position long, extending across the width of a paper or magnetic tape perpendicular to its movement. Several bit or punch positions may be included in a single frame through the use of different recording positions across the width of the tape.

full adder A computer circuit capable of adding three binary bits one of which is a "carry" from a previous addition.

full duplex Pertaining to the simultaneous, independent transmission of data in both directions over a communications link. Contrast with *half duplex* and *simplex*.

function (1) A process that is performed on a number or

84

character string; e.g., squaring is the mathematical function of multiplying a number by itself. (2) A precoded routine.

functional design The specification of the working relations between the parts of a system in terms of their characteristic actions.

functional units of a computer The organization of digital computers into five functional units: arithmetic unit, storage unit, control unit, input unit, and output unit.

fusible link A widely used *PROM* programming technique. An excessive current is used to destroy a metallized connection in a storage device, creating a zero, or instance, if a conducting element is interpreted as a 1.

G

gain The increase or amplification of a signal as it passes through a control system. Opposite of *attenuation*.

game theory A branch of mathematics concerned, among other things, with probability. The term was first used by John von Neumann in 1928 to describe the strategy of winning at poker. A mathematical process of selecting an optimum strategy in the face of an opponent who has a strategy of his own.

gang punch To punch identical or constant information into all of a group of punch cards.

gap See *interblock gap.*

garbage (1) A term often used to describe incorrect answers from a computer program, usually resulting from equipment malfunction or a mistake in a computer program. (2) Unwanted and meaningless data carried in storage. (3) Incorrect input to a computer. See *GIGO.*

garbage collection Loosely, a term for cleaning dead storage locations out of a file.

gate (1) An electronic circuit designed to produce an output under specific conditions, such as the AND gate, which requires both inputs to be present; and the OR gate, which requires either of two inputs to be present to produce an output. See *AND gate* and *OR gate*. (2) The control input terminal or electrode of a Field Effect Transistor (FET) or a Silicon Controlled Rectifier (SCR). See *drain* and *source*.

general-purpose Being applicable to a wide variety of uses without essential modification. Contrasted with *special-purpose*.

general-purpose computer A computer that is designed to solve a wide class of problems. The majority of digital computers are of this type. Contrast with special-purpose computer. See *digital computer*.

general-purpose register A CPU register used for indexing, addressing, and arithmetic and logical operations.

generalized routine A routine designed to process a large range of specific jobs within a given type of application.

generate (1) To use a generator to prepare a machine language program from a set of specifications. (2) To create new data from input information.

generation (of computers) A term usually applied to the progression of computers from those using vacuum tubes (*first generation*) to those using transistors (*second generation*), and to those using integrated circuits (*third generation*).

generator A computer program that constructs other programs to perform a particular type of operation; e.g., a report program generator, I/O generator.

geocoding A method of providing a graphic display of data in relation to a geographic area.

get To obtain a record from an input file.

GIGO An acronym for Garbage In-Garbage Out. A term used to describe the data into and out of a computer system — that is, if the input data is bad (Garbage In) then the output data will also be bad (Garbage Out).

glitch A sudden, often unexplained, electronic surge which causes problems in an electronic device.

global variable A variable that has the same value regardless of where or in what program it is used.

GP An acronym for General Purpose.

GPSS An acronym for General Purpose Systems

Simulation. A problem-oriented language used to develop simulation systems.

grabber A fixture on the end of a test equipment lead wire, with a spring actuated hook and claw designed to connect the measuring instrument to a pin of an integrated circuit, socket, transistor, etc.

gram A metric unit of mass weight equal to 1/1000 kilogram.

grammatical mistake A violation of the rules of use of a given programming language.

grandfather file See *father file*.

graphics Facilities to provide computer output in the form of displays, drawings, and pictures.

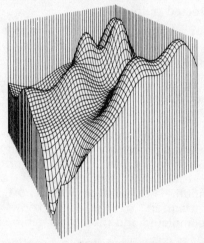

gray code A code which has the characteristic that successive integers differ from one another by only one digit. This is advantageous in analog-to-digital conversion equipment. Gray code is used only for input-output purposes. The coded values must be converted to binary before arithmetic calculations can be performed. Also called *cyclic code* and *reflected code*.

group mark Any indicator to signal the end of a word or other unit of data.

grouping Arranging data into related groups, having common characteristics.

gulp A small group of bytes.

H

half adder A computer circuit capable of adding two binary bits.

halfword A contiguous sequence of bits, bytes or characters which comprises half a computer word and is capable of being addressed as a unit. See *word*.

halt instruction A machine instruction which stops the execution of the program.

hamming code A 7-bit error-correcting data code capable of being corrected automatically.

hand calculator A small, hand-held calculator suitable for performing arithmetic operations and other more complicated calculations.

handler A program with the sole function of controlling a particular input, output, or storage device, a file, or the interrupt facility.

handshaking A term describing a pulse exchange between the central processing unit (CPU) and a peripheral device communicating in an asynchronous mode. Handshaking establishes synchronization and assures proper operation. Peripheral devices report their status during data transfers so the CPU knows when the operation is completed and more data can be transferred.

hang-up A nonprogrammed stop in a routine. It is usually an unforeseen or unwanted halt in a machine run. It is often caused by improper coding of a problem, equipment malfunction or by the attempted use of a nonexistent or illegal operation code.

hard copy A printed copy of machine output in readable form, for example, reports, listings, documents, summaries.

hard sector Magnetic floppy discs are divided into wedges called sectors which are physically marked by holes punched through the disc to indicate the various sectors. Soft sectoring is a method of determining position of data on the disc by software calculations rather than physical monitoring of the disc.

hardware Physical equipment such as electronic, magnetic, and mechanical devices. Contrast with *software*.

hardware resources CPU time, internal storage space, direct access storage space, and input/output devices, all of which are required to do the work of processing data automatically and efficiently.

hashing A key-to-address transformation in which the keys determine the location of the data.

head A device that reads, records or erases data on a storage medium, e.g., a small electromagnet used to read, write, or erase data on a magnetic disk.

header The first part of a message containing all the necessary information for directing the message to its destination(s).

header card A card that contains information about the data in cards that follow.

hertz Cycles per second. Abbreviated Hz.

heuristic Descriptive of an exploratory method of attacking a problem, in which the solution is obtained by successive evaluations of the progress toward the final results; e.g., guided trial and error. Contrast with *algorithm*. See *artificial intelligence* and *machine learning*.

hexadecimal Pertaining to a numeral system with a radix of 16. Digits greater than "9" are represented by letters of the alphabet. For example, the binary numeral 1110001011010011 can be represented as hexadecimal E2D3.

hexadecimal number A numeral, usually of more than one digit, representing a sum in which the quantity represented by each digit is based on a radix of sixteen. The digits used are 0,1,2,3,4,5,6,7,8,9,A,B,C,D,E, and F.

hexadecimal point The radix point in a hexadecimal numeral system. The point that separates the integer part of a mixed hexadecimal numeral from the fractional part. In the numeral 3F.6A7 the hexadecimal point is between the digits F and 6.

HI address byte The eight most significant bits in the 16-bit memory address word for the 8080 microprocessor. Abbreviated H or HI.

hierarchy (1) Order in which the arithmetic operations,

within a formula, or statement, will be executed. (2) Arrangement into a graded series.

high level language See *higher level language*.

high order Pertaining to the digit or digits of a number that have the greatest weight or significance; e.g., in the number 7643215, the high order digit is 7. Contrast with *low order*. See *most significant digit*.

high order column The leftmost column of a punch card field.

high speed printer See *line printer*.

higher level language A programming language oriented toward the problem to be solved or the procedures to be used. Contrast with *machine language*. See *problem-oriented language* and *procedure-oriented language*.

hit A successful comparison of two items of data. Contrast with *match*.

holding time In data communications, the length of time a communication channel is in use for each transmission. Includes both message time and operating time.

Hollerith, Herman (1860-1929) As a statistician and employee of the Census Bureau he proposed using punched cards in conjunction with electromechanical relays to accomplish simple additions and sortings needed in the 1890 census. He set up a company to manufacture his punched card tabulator, and it became one of the parents of IBM Corporation.

Hollerith card A punched card consisting of 80 columns, each of which is divided from top to bottom into 12 punching positions.

Hollerith code A particular type of code used to represent alphanumeric data on punched cards. Named after Herman Hollerith, the originator of punched card tabulating. Each card column holds one character, and each decimal digit, letter, and special character is represented by one, two, or three holes punched into designated row positions of the column.

holographic storage Uses the laser beam to create images for computer storage. See *laser*.

home computer A small low cost microcomputer introduced during the mid-1970's. Many vendors and computer stores who sell home computers also offer them in kit form. Sometimes called *personal computer*. See *computer kit* and *microcomputer*.

Pharmacists at this hospital are filling prescriptions with the help of a computer. When a prescription is received in the pharmacy, a drug code is entered into the computer via a TV-like terminal with information on the patient and doctor. The information is reviewed by the computer, and if not challenged in any way, a nearby printer types out a label to be affixed to the prescription.

home record The first record in a chain of records used with the chaining method of file organization.

hopper See *card hopper.*

housekeeping Computer operations that do not directly contribute toward the desired results; in general, initialization, set-up and clean-up operations. Sometimes called *bookkeeping.*

HSP An acronym for *High Speed Printer.*

hybrid computer A data processing device that uses both analog and digital data representation.

hybrids Circuits fabricated by interconnecting smaller circuits of different technologies mounted on a single substrate.

hypertape A magnetic tape unit that uses a cartridge rather than a reel of tape. The cartridge consists of a reel of tape and the take-up reel.

hysteresis The lag in a process response when a force acting on it is abruptly changed. Hysteresis may be caused by various mechanical, electrical, or physical conditions, and may or may not be desirable.

Hz An abbreviation for hertz; cycles per second.

I

IBM Corporation The world's largest manufacturer of data processing equipment.

IC An acronym for *Integrated Circuit,* a complex electronic circuit fabricated on a single piece of material, usually a silicon chip.

ICE An acronym for In-Circuit Emulator. A device which is plugged directly into the user's system in a real time environment. It is used to control, interrogate, revise, and completely debug a user's system in its own environment.

ICES An acronym for Integrated Civil Engineering System. A system developed to aid civil engineers in solving engineering problems. ICES consists of several engineering systems and programming languages.

identifier A symbol whose purpose is to identify, indicate, or name a body of data.

idle time The time that a computer system is available for use, but is not in actual operation.

IDP An acronym for *Integrated Data Processing.*

IEEE An acronym for Institute of Electrical and Electronics Engineers. A professional engineering organization with a strong interest in computer systems and their uses.

IFIPS An acronym for International Federation of Information Processing Societies. An international computer organization.

I²L An acronym for Integrated Injection Logic. I²L chips are used in electronic wristwatches, and as control devices for industrial products, automobiles, and computer systems.

illegal character A character or combination of bits which is not accepted as a valid or known representation by the computer.

illegal operation A process which the computer cannot perform.

image An exact logical duplicate stored in a different medium. See *card image.*

immediate access Ability of a computer to put data in (or remove it from) storage without delay.

immediate access storage See *internal storage.*

immediate address Pertaining to an instruction whose address part contains the value of an operand rather than its address. It is not an address at all, but rather an operand supplied as part of an instruction.

impact printer A data printout device that imprints by

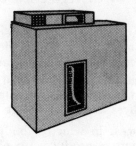

momentary pressure of raised type against paper, using ink or ribbon as a color medium. See *line printer.*

implementation (1) The process of installing a computer system. It involves choosing the equipment, installing the equipment, personnel training, and establishing computing center operating policies. (2) The representation of a programming language on a specific computer system; e.g., the version of FORTRAN available on the XYZ computer.

inclusive OR The Boolean operator which gives a truth table value of true if either or both of the two variables it connects is true. If neither is true, the value is false.

increment An amount added to or subtracted from a value of a variable.

incremental plotter See *plotter.*

index (1) A symbol or number used to identify a particular quantity in an array of similar quantities; for example, X(5) is the fifth item in an array of X's. (2) A table of references, held in storage in some sequence, which may be addressed to obtain the addresses of other items of data; e.g., items in a file. See *index register.*

index register A register whose contents can be added to or subtracted from an address prior to or during the execution of an instruction.

indexed address An address that is modified by the content of an index register prior to or during the execution of a computer instruction.

indexed sequential access method A means of organizing data on a direct access device. A directory or index is created to show where the data records are stored. Any desired data record can thus be retrieved from the device by consulting the index(es).

indicator A device which registers a condition in the computer.

indirect address An address that specifies a storage location that contains either a direct address or another indirect address. Also called *multilevel addressing.*

induce To produce an electrical charge, current, or voltage by induction. A charge on the gate of a field effect transistor (FET) induces an equal charge in the channel.

induction The process in which a body having electric and magnetic properties produces an electric charge, a voltage, or a magnetic field in an adjacent body, without physical contact.

inherent   An instruction addressing mode in the Motorola MC6800 microprocessor that is equivalent to immediate addressing.

information   Meaningful and useful facts that are extracted from data fed to a computer. The meaning assigned to data by known conventions.

information explosion   The exponential increase in the growth and diversification of all forms of information.

information management system   A system designed to organize, catalog, locate, store, retrieve, and maintain information.

information networks   The interconnection of a geographically dispersed group of libraries and information centers, through telecommunications, for the purpose of sharing their total information resources among more people.

information processing   The totality of operations performed by a computer; the handling of data according to rules of procedure to accomplish operations such as classifying, sorting, calculating, and recording. Same as *data processing*.

information processing center   See *data processing center*.

information retrieval (1) That branch of computer technology concerned with techniques for storing and searching large quantities of data and making selected data available. (2) The methods used to recover specific information from stored data.

information science   The study of how people create, use, and communicate information in all forms.

information storage and retrieval   See *information retrieval*.

information system   A formal method by which information can be found, delivered, and used by those who need it.

information theory   The branch of learning concerned with the likelihood of accurate transmission or communication of messages subject to transmission failure, noise, and distortion.

information utility   See *computer utility*.

inhibit To prohibit from taking place.

initialize To preset a variable or counter to proper starting values before commencing a calculation. See *preset*.

in-line coding Coding which is located in the main part of a routine.

in-line processing The processing of data in random order, not subject to preliminary editing or sorting.

input The introduction of data from an external storage medium into a computer's internal storage unit. Contrast with *output*.

input area An area of internal storage reserved for input data (data transferred from an input device or an auxiliary storage device). Contrast with *output area*.

input data Data to be processed. Synonymous with *input*. Contrast with *output data*.

input device A unit which is used to get data into the central processing unit from the human user. Card readers, typewriters, MICR units, and acoustic character recognition (voice input) units are examples of input devices. Contrast with *output device*.

input job stream See *job stream*.

input/output Pertaining to the techniques, media, and devices used to achieve human/machine communication. Abbreviated I/O.

input/output channel A channel that transmits input data to, or output data from, a computer. See *multiplexor channel* and *selector channel*.

input/output control system A set of routines for handling the many detailed aspects of input and output operations; commonly abbreviated IOCS.

input/output device A unit which is used to get data into the central processing unit from the human user, and to transfer data from the computer's internal storage to some storage or output device. See *input device, output device* and *peripheral equipment*.

input/output symbol A flowcharting symbol used to indicate an input operation to the procedure or an output operation from the procedure. A parallelogram figure is used to represent this symbol.

input stream The sequence of control statements and data submitted to the operating system on an input unit especially activated for that purpose by the operator. Same as *job stream*.

inquiry A request for data from storage; e.g., a request for the number of available airline seats in an airline reservation system.

inquiry station The device from which any inquiry is made.

insertion method See *sifting*.

installation A general term for a particular computing system, in the context of the overall function it serves and the individuals who manage it, operate it, apply it to problems, service it, and use the results it produces.

installation time Time spent in installing, testing, and accepting equipment.

instruction A group of characters, bytes or bits that defines an operation to be performed by the computer. See *machine instruction*.

instruction code Same as *operation code*.

instruction counter A counter that indicates the location of the next computer instruction to be interpreted.

instruction format The makeup and arrangement of a computer instruction.

instruction register A hardware register that stores an instruction for execution.

instruction set A set of vendor-supplied operation codes for a particular computer or family of computers. Synonymous with *repertoire*.

instruction time The time it takes for an instruction to be fetched from internal storage by the control unit and interpreted.

instruction word A computer word which contains an instruction.

instructional computing The educational process of teaching individuals the various phases of computer science/data processing.

integer A whole number which may be positive, negative or zero. It does not have a fractional part. Examples of integers are 26, -417, and 0.

integrated circuit A complete solid-state circuit, usually highly compact, produced by mass-production methods. An integrated circuit is capable of performing all the functions of a conventional circuit containing numerous discrete transistors, diodes, capacitors, and/or resistors, all of whose component parts are fabricated and assembled in a single integrated process. An integrated circuit may contain anywhere from a few to thousands of transistors, capacitors, diodes, etc. See *large scale integration (LSI)*, *medium scale integration (MSI)* and *small scale integration (SSI)*.

integrated data processing Data processing by a system that coordinates a number of previously unconnected processes in order to improve overall efficiency by reducing or eliminating redundant data entry or processing operations. Abbreviated IDP.

integrated injection logic See *I²L*.

intelligence See *artificial intelligence*.

intelligent terminal An input/output device in which a number of computer processing characteristics are physically built into, or attached to, the terminal unit. See *point-of-sale terminal*.

interactive processing A type of real-time processing involving a continuing dialog between user and computer; the user is allowed to modify data and/or instructions. See *conversational mode*.

interactive system A system in which the human user or device serviced by the computer can communicate directly with the operating program. For human users, this is termed a conversational system.

interblock gap The distance on a magnetic tape between the end of one block and the beginning of the next. Such spacing facilitates tape start-stop operations. Also called *interrecord gap* and *record gap*.

interface A common boundary between two pieces of hardware or between two systems.

interference Unwanted signals which degrade the quality of wanted signals.

interlace To assign successive addresses to physically separated storage locations on a magnetic disk or drum in such a way as to reduce the access time.

interleaving A multiprogramming technique, in which parts of one program are inserted into another program, so that if there are processing delays in one of the programs, parts of the other program can be processed.

interlock A protective facility that prevents one device or operation from interfering with another; for example, the locking of the switches on the control console to prevent manual movement of the switches while the computer is executing a program.

intermittent error An error which occurs intermittently but not constantly and is extremely difficult to reproduce.

internal memory Same as *internal storage*.

internal sort The sequencing of two or more records within the central processing unit. The first phase of a multipass sort program.

internal storage Addressable storage directly controlled by the central processing unit. The central processing unit uses internal storage to store programs while they are being executed and data while it is being processed. Also called *immediate access storage, internal memory, main storage* and *primary storage*.

interpreter (1) A computer program that translates each source language statement into a sequence of machine instructions and then executes these machine instructions before translating the next source language statement. (2) A device that prints on a punched card the data already punched in the card.

interrecord gap Same as *interblock gap*.

interrupt A signal which when activated causes the hardware to transfer program control to some specific location in internal storage thus breaking the normal flow of the program being executed. After the interrupt has been processed, program control is again returned to the interrupted program. An interrupt can be generated as the result of a program action, by an operator activating switches on the computer console, or by a peripheral device causing the interrupting signal. Often called a *trap*.

inventory management A term applied to the daily and periodic bookkeeping commonly associated with inventory control and forecasting the future needs of items or groups of items.

inverted file   A file organized so that it can be accessed by character rather than record key.

inverter   A circuit in which a binary one input produces a binary zero output and vice versa.

I/O   An abbreviation for *input/output*.

I/O bound   The term applied to programs that require a large number of input/output operations, resulting in much central processing unit wait time. Contrast with *compute bound*.

IOCS   An acronym for Input/Output Control System. A standard set of input/output routines designed to initiate and control the input and output processes of a computer system.

IPL   (1) An acronym for Initial Programming Loading. The process of loading the operating system into storage. (2) An acronym for Information Processing Language. A list-processing language primarily used for working with heuristic type problems.

ISAM   An acronym for *Indexed Sequential Access Method*.

ISO   An acronym for International Organization for Standardization.

ISR   An acronym for Information Storage and Retrieval. See *information retrieval*.

item   A group of related characters treated as a unit. (A record is a group of related items, and a file is a group of related records).

iterate   To repeat, automatically, under program control, the same series of processing steps until a predetermined stop or branch condition is reached. See *loop* and *Newton-Raphson*.

J

jack   A connecting device to which a wire or wires of a circuit may be attached and which is arranged for the insertion of a plug.

Jacquard loom A weaving machine invented near the beginning of the 19th century by Joseph Marie Jacquard in which punched cards controlled the movements of the shuttles in order to produce tapestries of complicated design.

jargon The technical vocabulary associated with a specific trade, business or profession.

job A collection of specified tasks constituting a unit of work for a computer; e.g., a program or related group of programs used as a unit.

job control language The language used in control cards. Cards representing job control language are interspersed with source or object card decks and data decks. These cards give information concerning who the computer user is, what charge number to use, etc. See *control cards.*

job queue The set of programs and data currently making its way through the computer. In most operating systems, each job is brought into the queue and is processed (given control of the computer) when it is the "oldest" job within its own priority. An exception to this is the case of a job of higher priority which has not yet obtained sufficient resources to be processed.

job stream The input to the operating system; may consist of one or more jobs. Same as *input stream.*

job-to-job transition The process of locating a program, the files associated with the program, and preparing the computer for the execution of a particular job.

JOVIAL An acronym for Jules' Own Version of the International Algorithmetic Language. A programming language used primarily for working with scientific, and command and control problems. The language has wide usage in systems implemented by the U.S. Air Force.

jump A departure from the normal sequence of executing instructions in a computer. Synonymous with *branch* and *transfer.* See *conditional transfer* and *unconditional transfer.*

justification The act of adjusting, arranging, or shifting digits to the left or right, to fit a prescribed pattern.

justify To align the characters in a field. For example, to left justify, the first character (e.g., the *most significant digit*) appears in the leftmost character position in a field. To right justify, the last character (e.g., the *least significant digit*) is written in the last or rightmost character position in the field. See *normalize.*

juxtaposition The positioning of items adjacent to each other.

K

K (1) An abbreviation for kilo or 1000 in decimal notation. For example, "100K ch/s" means "a reading speed of 100 000 characters per second." (2) Loosely, when referring to storage capacity — two to the tenth power; in decimal notation 1024. The expression 8K represents 8192 (8 times 1024).

kc One thousand characters per second. Used to express the rate of data transfer operations.

kelvin The unit of temperature measurement of the SI metric system, for normal use expressed in degrees celsius.

key (1) The field or fields which identify a record. (2) The field which determines the position of a record in a sorted sequence. (3) A lever on a manually operated machine, such as a typewriter, teletypewriter, or keypunch.

key verification See *card verification.*

keyboard A group of marked levers operated manually for recording characters.

keyboard-to-disk system A data entry system in which data can be entered directly onto a disk by typing the data into a keyboard.

keyboard-to-tape system A system in which data can be entered directly onto a tape by typing the data at a keyboard.

keypunch A keyboard operated device used to punch holes in punch cards to represent data.

keypunching The process by which original, or source data is recorded in punch cards. The operator reads source documents and, by depressing keys on a keypunch machine, converts source document information into punched holes.

keystroke The action of pressing one of the keys on a keyboard.

key-verify The use of the punch card machine known as a verifier, which has a keyboard, to make sure that the information supposed to be punched in a punch card has actually been properly punched. The machine indicates when the punched hole and the depressed key disagree. See *verifier machine*.

keyword (1) One of the significant and informative words in a title or document which describe the content of that document. (2) A primary element in a programming language statement; e.g., words such as LET, GOTO, and INPUT in the BASIC programming language.

kilo Metric prefix, means 1000 times.

kilobit A thousand bits.

kilobyte A kilobyte is 2^{10} or 1024 bytes. It is commonly abbreviated to "K" and used as a suffix when describing memory size. Thus, 24K really means a $24 \times 1024 = 24,576$ byte memory system.

kilocycle One thousand cycles per second.

kilomegacycle A billion cycles per second.

kludge An ill-assorted collection of poorly matching parts, loosely fit together to form a distressing whole.

KSR An acronym for Keyboard Send/Receive. A teletypewriter unit with keyboard and printer.

L

label An identifier or name which is used in a computer program to identify or describe an instruction, statement, message, data value, record, item, or file. Same as *name*.

language A set of rules, representations, and conventions used to convey information.

language statement A statement that is coded by a user of a computing system, and is used to convey information to a processing program such as a language translator program, service program, or control program. A statement may signify that an operation be performed or may simply contain data that is to be passed to the processing program.

language subset A part of a language that can be used independently of the rest of the language.

language translation The process or changing information from one language to another — for example, Russian to English, English to German, BASIC to FORTRAN, or COBOL to PL/I.

language translator A program that transforms statements from one language to another without significantly changing their meaning; e.g., a *compiler* or *assembler*.

large scale integration (LSI) An integrated circuit that contains a large number of transistors and other circuitry on a single chip. LSI chips are small; however, they are slower operating than bipolar logic, such as transistor-transistor logic (TTL). LSI chips are used in microprocessors, microcomputers and other larger machines. See *metallic oxide semiconductor*.

laser A tightly packed, narrow beam of light formed by the emission of high-energy molecules. See *holographic storage*.

latency The time between the completion of the interpretation of an address and the start of the actual transfer from the addressed location. Latency includes the delay associated with access to storage devices such as magnetic disks and magnetic drums.

leader A blank section of tape at the beginning of a reel of paper tape or magnetic tape.

leading edge The edge of a punched card which first enters the card reader.

leased line Generally refers to a private full-period data communication line.

least significant digit Pertaining to the digit of a number that has the least weight or significance; e.g., in the number 54321, the least significant digit is 1. Abbreviated LSD. See *justify* and *low order.*

LED An acronym for Light Emitting Diode, a commonly used alphanumeric display unit which glows when supplied with a specified voltage.

left justify See *justify.*

Leibniz, Baron von (1646-1716) A German mathematician who invented a calculating machine called a "stepped reckoner" (in 1672) which could add, subtract, and multiply. The machine performed addition and subtraction in the same manner as Pascal's machine; however, additional gears were included in the machine which enabled it to multiply directly.

length As related to a computer word — the number of characters, bytes, or bits in a computer word. A variable word is made up of several characters ending with a special end character. A fixed word is composed of the same number of bits, bytes, or characters in each word. See *fixed word length* and *variable word length.*

level The degree of subordination in a hierarchy.

lexicon A language with definitions for all terms.

library A published collection of programs, routines and subroutines available to every user of the computer. Same as *program library.* See *disk library* and *tape library.*

library automation Application of computers and other technology to library operations and services.

library routine A tested routine that is maintained in a program library.

LIFO An acronym for Last In-First Out, the way most microprocessor program stacks operate. The last data or instruction word placed on the stack is the first to be retrieved. See *pushdown list.*

light emitting diode See *LED.*

light pen An electrical device that resembles a pen and can be used to write or sketch on the screen of a cathode ray tube; that is, to provide input to the computer through its use.

line See *channel*.

line printer An output peripheral device which prints data one line at a time. See *electrostatic printer*.

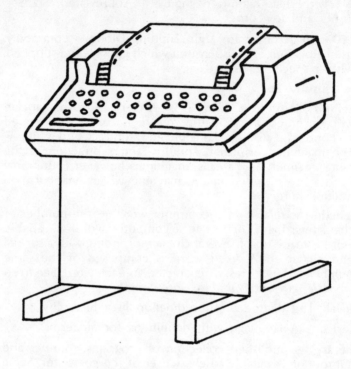

A line printer.

line printing The printing of an entire line of characters as a unit.

line speed The maximum rate at which signals may be transmitted over a given channel; usually in baud or bits per second.

linear programming Technique for finding an optimum combination, when there may be no single best one. For example, linear programming could be used to solve the problem: "What combination of foods would give the most calories and best nutrition for the least money?" A computer need not be used; often it is because such problems would take too long to solve by hand. Abbreviated LP.

link In data communications, a physical connection between one location and another whose function is to transmit data. See *communication channel.*

linkage Coding that connects two separately coded routines; e.g., the coding that links a subroutine to the program with which it is to be used. See *calling sequence.*

linking loader An executive program that connects different program segments so they may be run in the computer as one unit. A useful piece of software that makes subtasks easily available to a main task.

liquid crystal display An electro luminescent technology used in alphanumeric and other digital displays.

LISP An acronym for LISt Processing. A list processing language primarily designed to process data consisting of lists.

list (1) Organization of data using indexes and pointers to allow for nonsequential retrieval. (2) An ordered set of items. (3) To print every relevant item of input data. (4) A system command to print program statements; e.g., the LIST command in the BASIC language will cause the system to print a listing of the program.

list processing A method of processing data in the form of lists. Usually, chained lists are used so that the logical order of items can be changed without altering their physical locations.

listing Generally, any report produced on a printing device (line printer or typewriter). For example, a source listing is a printout of the source program processed by the compiler; an error listing is a report showing all input data found to be invalid by the processing program. See *assembly listing.*

liter A metric unit of liquid capacity equal to one cubic decimeter.

literal Another name for *constant.*

liveware Revolting (and misleading) expression meaning computer people.

LO address byte The eight least significant bits in the 16-bit memory address word for the 8080 microprocessor.

load (1) To read information into the storage of a computer. (2) To put cards into a card reader, to put a paper tape onto a paper tape reader, or to put a disk pack on a disk drive unit.

load-and-go An operating technique in which the loading and execution phases of a program are performed in one continuous run. See *compile-and-go.*

load point A spot at the beginning of a tape.

load sharing The technique of using two or more computers in order to handle excess volumes during peak periods. It is desirable to have one computer handle less than peak loads with the others acting as the fall-back equipment.

loader A service routine designed to read programs into internal storage in preparation for their execution.

location Loosely, anyplace in which data may be stored. See *storage location.*

lock code A sequence of letters and/or numbers provided by the operators of a time sharing system to prevent unauthorized tampering with a user's program. The lock code serves as a secret "password" in that the computer will refuse any changes to the program unless the user supplies the correct lock code.

lockout (1) Suppression of an interrupt. (2) A programming technique used to prevent access to critical data by both CPU's at the same time (in a multiprocessing environment).

log A record of the operations of data processing equipment, listing each job or run, the time it required, operator actions, and other pertinent data.

logarithm The exponent of the power to which a fixed number is to be raised to produce a given number. The fixed number is called the base and is usually 10 or e. Example: $2^3 = 8$, 3 is the logarithm of 8 to the base 2; which means that 2 must be raised to the third power to produce 8.

logging-in The process of establishing communication with and verifying the authority to use the computer during conversational programming. See *conversational mode.*

logic (1) The science dealing with the formal principles of reasoning and thought. (2) The basic principles and application of truth tables and interconnection between logical elements required for arithmetic computation in an automatic data processing system.

logic circuits A series of flip-flops and gates that direct electrical impulses to and from the appropriate portions of a computer system.

logic diagram A diagram that represents a logical design and sometimes the hardware implementation.

logic element A device that performs a logic function.

logic symbol A symbol used to represent a logic element graphically.

logical decision Generally a decision as to which one of two possible courses of action is to be followed.

logical design The specification of the working relations between the parts of a system in terms of symbolic logic and without primary regard for hardware implementation.

logical file A collection of one or more logical records. See *logical record.*

logical instruction An instruction that executes an operation that is defined in symbolic logic, such as AND, OR, or NOR.

logical operations The computer operations which are logical in nature, such as logical tests and decisions. This is in contrast with the arithmetic and data transfer operations, which involve no decision.

logical product The AND function of several terms. The product is 1 only when all of the terms are 1, otherwise it is 0.

logical record The record as defined by the program designer. One or more logical records are normally stored in a physical record. Contrast with *physical record.*

logical sum The Inclusive OR function of several terms. The sum is 1 when any or all of the terms are 1; and it is 0 only when all are 0.

logical unit number A number assigned to a physical peripheral device.

logical value A value which may be either "true" or "false" depending on the result of a particular logical decision.

LOGO A higher level, interactive programming language

that assumes the user has access to some type of on-line terminal. The language was developed at M.I.T. by Seymour Papert and his co-workers. The language was designed for school students and seems particularly suited to students in the younger age groups.

look-up See *table look-up.*

loop A sequence of instructions in a program that can be executed repetitively until certain specified conditions are satisfied. See closed loop.

loop code The repetition of a sequence of instructions by using a program loop. Loop coding requires more execution time than would straight line coding but will result in a savings of storage.

looping Executing the same instruction or series of instructions over and over again.

low level language A machine-dependent programming language translated by an assembler into instructions and data formats for a given machine. Same as *assembly language.*

low order Pertaining to the digit or digits of a number that have the least weight or significance; e.g., in the number 7643215, the low order digit is 5. Contrast with *high order.* See *least significant digit.*

low order column The rightmost (highest numbered) column of a punch card field.

LP An acronym for *Linear Programming.*

LPM An acronym for Lines Per Minute.

LSC An acronym for Least Significant Character.

LPM An acronym for *Lines Per Minute.*

LSC An acronym for *Least Significant Character.*

LSD An acronym for *Least Significant Digit.*

LSI An acronym for *Large Scale Integration.*

M

machine address Same as *absolute address.*

machine code An operation code that a machine is designed to recognize.

machine error A deviation from correctness in data resulting from an equipment failure.

machine independent (1) A term used to indicate that a program is developed in terms of the problem rather than in terms of the characteristics of the computer system. (2) The ability to run a program on the computers made by different manufacturers, or upon the various machines made by the same manufacturer.

machine instruction An instruction that a computer can directly recognize and execute. See *instruction.*

machine language The basic language of a computer. Programs written in machine language requires no further interpretation by a computer.

machine learning Refers to a heuristic process where a device improves its performance based on past actions. See *artificial intelligence* and *heuristic.*

machine operator See *computer operator.*

machine oriented language A programming language that is more like a machine language than a human language.

machine-readable information Information recorded on any medium in such a way that it can be sensed or read by a machine. Also called *machine-sensible.*

machine run See *run.*

machine-sensible See *machine-readable information.*

macro assembler An assembler that allows the user to create and define new computer instructions (called macros).

macro instruction (1) A source language instruction that is equivalent to a specified number of machine language instructions. (2) A machine language instruction that is composed of several micro instructions.

macro programming Programming with macro instructions; e.g., writing control programs for a microprocessor using macro instructions. See *macro instruction* and *micro instruction*.

mag tape A term sometimes used instead of magnetic tape.

magnetic Of, producing, caused by, or operated by magnetism.

magnetic bubble memory A memory that uses magnetic "bubbles" that move. The bubbles are locally-magnetized areas that can move about in a magnetic material, such as a plate of orthoferrite. It is possible to control the reading in and out of this "bubble" within the magnetic material and, as a result, a very high-capacity memory can be built. Small bubble memory chips have been developed for use in microcomputer systems. Widespread usage of bubble memory chips can be expected within the immediate future.

magnetic card A storage device consisting of a tray or cartridge of magnetically coated cards. These cards are made of similar material to magnetic tape (although considerably thicker) and have specific areas allocated for storing information. A magnetic card may be visualized as a magnetic tape cut into strips; several strips are placed side by side on a plastic card and mounted in a cartridge. See *CRAM* and *data cell*.

magnetic characters A set of characters that is used for checks, insurance billings, utility bills, invoices, and so forth, that permit special character-reading devices (MICR readers) to be employed to read the characters automatically. See *magnetic ink character recognition*.

magnetic core A tiny doughnut-shaped piece of magnetizable material capable of storing one binary digit.

magnetic core plane A network of magnetic cores, each of which represents one core common to each storage location. A number of core planes are stacked together to form a magnetic core storage unit.

magnetic core storage A system of storage in which data are represented in binary form by means of the directional flow of magnetic fields in tiny doughnut-shaped arrays of magnetic cores.

magnetic disk A peripheral storage device in which data is recorded on magnetizable disk surfaces. See *fixed disk unit, disk pack, floppy disk, direct access,* and *moveable-head disk unit.*

magnetic drum A peripheral storage device consisting of a cylinder with a magnetizable surface on which data is recorded. See *direct access*.

magnetic film storage A storage device that uses 35 mm magnetic film which is contained on a spool. The spool may be loaded on to a film handler unit.

magnetic head A device which is used for reading and writing information on devices such as magnetic tapes, disks, or drums.

magnetic ink An ink that contains particles of a magnetic substance whose presence can be detected by magnetic sensors.

magnetic ink character recognition The recognition of characters printed with a special magnetic ink by machines. Abbreviated MICR.

magnetic resonance The phenomenon in which a movement of a particle or system of particles is coupled resonantly to an external magnetic field.

magnetic storage Utilizing the magnetic properties of materials to store data on such devices and media as disks, tapes, cards, drums, cores, and films.

magnetic tape A plastic tape having a magnetic surface for storing data in a code of magnetized spots. Data may be represented on tape using a six- or eight-bit coding structure.

magnetic tape cassette A magnetic tape storage device. A cassette consists of a magnetic tape housed in a plastic container.

magnetic tape cartridge A magnetic tape contained in a cartridge. The cartridge consists of a reel of tape and the take-up reel.

magnetic tape code The system of coding which is used to record magnetized patterns on magnetic tape. The magnetized patterns represent alphanumeric data. See *BCD* and *EBCDIC*.

magnetic tape deck Same as *magnetic tape unit*.

magnetic tape density The number of characters that can be recorded on 2.54 cm (1 inch) of magnetic tape. A common recording density for magnetic tape is 1600 characters per inch.

magnetic tape drive   A device that moves tape past a head. Synonymous with *magnetic tape transport.*

magnetic tape reel   A reel used to preserve the physical charactristics of magnetic tape. The tape is usually 1.27 cm (½ inch) wide and 751.52 meters (2400 feet) in length.

magnetic tape sorting   A sort program that utilizes magnetic tapes for auxiliary storage during a sort.

magnetic tape transport   Same as *magnetic tape drive.*

magnetic tape unit   A device containing a magnetic tape drive, together with reading and writing heads and associated controls. Synonymous with *magnetic tape deck.* See *magnetic tape cassette* and *magnetic tape cartridge.*

magnetic thin film   See *thin film.*

magnitude   (1) The absolute value of a number. (2) Size.

mail box   A set of locations in a RAM storage area. An area reserved for data addressed to specific peripheral devices or other microprocessors.

main frame   Same as *central processing unit.*

main storage   The fastest general purpose storage of a computer. Same as *internal storage.*

maintainability   The characteristic associated with the isolation and repair of a failure.

maintenance   Tests, adjustments, repairs, or replacements that keep hardware and/or software in proper working order.

malfunction   A failure in the operation of the central processing unit or peripheral device. The effect of a *fault.* Contrast with *error* and *mistake.*

management   The individuals responsible for planning, organizing, and controlling a function or organization.

management information system   An information system designed to supply organizational managers with the necessary information needed to plan, organize, staff, direct, and control the operations of the organization. Abbreviated MIS.

mantissa   That part of a floating point number which specifies the significant digits of the number. For example, in .64321×10^3, .64321 is the mantissa.

manual operation   Processing of data in a system by direct manual techniques.

manufacturer's software A set of programming aids that the computer manufacturer supplies or makes available with a computer. See *systems programs*.

map A list that indicates the area of storage occupied by various elements of a program and its data. Also called *storage map*.

mapping A transformation from one set to another set; a correspondence.

marginal checking A preventive maintenance procedure in which the unit under test is varied from its normal value in an effort to detect and locate components which are operating in a marginal condition.

mark sensing The ability to mark cards or pages with an electrographic pencil to be read directly into the computer via a mark-sense reader. This is a very useful technique for acquiring data by hand and avoiding the time lag and inaccuracy of keypunching. See *optical mark reader*.

Mark I First electromechanical computer developed under the direction of Howard Aiken at Harvard University. Also called *ASCC (Automatic Sequence Controlled Calculator)*.

MASER An acronym for Microwave Amplification by the Stimulated Emission of Radiation. A device capable of amplifying or generating radio frequency radiation. Maser amplifiers are used in satellite communication ground stations to amplify the extremely weak signals received from communication satellites.

mask (1) A machine word containing a pattern of bits, bytes, or characters that is used to extract or select parts of other machine words by controlling an instruction which retains or eliminates selected bits, bytes, or characters. (2) In semiconductor fabrication, a photographically produced stencil used during semiconductor fabrication to control areas of metal deposition on the silicon chip, or to limit the regions of doping the diffusion process. (3) Photographically produced masks are used by semiconductor manufacturers to control the metallization pattern during the fabrication of ROM chips.

mass storage Same as *auxiliary storage* or *secondary storage*.

master clear A switch on some computer consoles that will clear certain operational registers and prepare for a new mode of operation.

master clock The device which controls the basic timing pulses of a computer.

master file A file containing relatively, permanent information which is used as a source of reference and is generally updated periodically. Contrast with *detail file*.

master-slave computer system A computer system consisting of a master computer connected to one or more slave computers. The master computer provides the scheduling function and jobs to the slave computer(s).

match To check for identity between two or more items of data. Contrast with *hit*.

matching A data processing operation where two files are checked to determine if there is a corresponding item or group of items in each file.

mathematical logic The use of mathematical symbols to represent language and its processes, in which these symbols are manipulated in accord with mathematical rules to determine whether or not a statement or a series of statements is true or false. See *logic*.

mathematical model A group of mathematical expressions which represents a process, a system, or the operation of a device. See *simulation*.

mathematics The study of relation between objects or quantities, organized so that certain facts can be proved or derived from others by using logic. See *applied mathematics*.

matrix A rectangular arrangment of elements (numbers or characters); each element requires two subscripts to identify it — the first identifies the row, the second, the column. See *array*.

matrix notation Introduced by the English mathematician Arthur Cayley in 1858. He used an abbreviated notation, such as AX = B for expressing systems of linear equations.

matrix printer A printer that uses a matrix of dots to form an image of the character being printed. A type of *line printer*.

Mauchly, John Co-inventor of the ENIAC, an early electronic computer.

mechanical data processing A method of data processing which involves the use of relatively small and simple (usually nonprogrammable) mechanical machines.

mechanical translation A generic term for language translation by computers or similar equipment.

media The plural form of medium.

medium The physical substance upon which data is recorded — for example, magnetic disk, paper tape, floppy disk, magnetic tape, punch cards, and paper.

medium scale integration The accumulation of several circuits (usually less than 100) on a single chip of semiconductor. Abbreviated MSI. See *TTL*.

mega A prefix indicating million.

megabit A million binary digits.

megacycle A million cycles per second.

megahertz A million cycles per second. Abbreviated MHz.

memory The storage facilities of the computer, capable of storing vast amounts of data. See *auxiliary storage, internal storage, PROM, RAM, ROM,* and *storage*.

memory allocation See *storage allocation*.

memory cycle See *cycle*.

memory dump See *storage dump*.

memory map See *storage map*.

memory protection See *storage protection*.

merge To combine items into one sequenced file from two or more similarly sequenced files without changing the order of the items. Same as *collate*.

message A group of characters having meaning as a whole and always handled as a group.

message format Rules for the placement of such portions of a message as message heading, address text, and end of message.

message header The leading part of a message that contains information concerning the message, such as the source or destination code of the message, the message priority, and the type of message.

message retrieval The capability to retrieve a message some time after it has entered an information system.

message switching The switching technique of receiving a message, storing it until the proper outgoing circuit and station are available and then retransmitting it toward its

117

destination. Computers are often used to perform the switching function.

message switching center A center in which messages are routed according to information contained within the messages themselves.

metacompiler A compiler for a langauge that is used primarily for writing compilers, usually syntax oriented compilers. A special-purpose metacompiler language is not very useful for writing general programs.

metalanguage A language which is used to describe a language.

metallic oxide semiconductor A process that is used in making LSI (large scale integration) chips. MOS chips are smaller; however, slower operating than bipolar logic, such as TTL (transistor-transistor logic). See *CMOS* and *large scale integration*.

meta-metalanguage A language which is used to describe a metalanguage.

meter Base unit of length in the SI metric system, approximately equal to 1.1 yards.

metric system Systeme International d'Unites or SI. The modern version of the metric system currently in wide use in the world. It is based on 7 base units: *meter, kilogram, second, ampere, kelvin* (degrees *celsius*), *candela,* and *mole.*

metric ton Measure of weight equal to 1000 kilograms or about 2200 pounds.

MFT An acronym for Multiprogramming with a Fixed number of Tasks; the tasks being programs. Sometimes called (jokingly, of course) Multiprogramming with a Finite amount of Trouble.

MHz An abbreviation for megahertz; million cycles per second.

MICR An acronym for Magnetic Ink Character Recognition.

micro One millionth, used as a prefix; for example, a microsecond is a millionth of a second.

micro code See *micro instruction.*

micro instruction A low level instruction used to obtain a macro, or machine language instruction.

microcoding Composing computer instructions by combining basic, elementary operations to form higher level instructions such as addition or multiplication. See *micro instruction.*

microcoding device Circuit board with fixed instructions for performing standard functions through miniature logic circuits, thus avoiding the need to code these instructions during programming.

microcomputer A small, low cost computer. A microcomputer contains at least one microprocessor. It functions much the same way as a minicomputer. Several manufacturers are offering microcomputers in kit form. See *computer kit, home computer, microcomputer chip, microprocessor* and *personal computer.*

A microcomputer.

microcomputer applications Microcomputers are finding applications in business, technology, industry, and the home. They are used in video game machines, traffic control systems, point-of-sale terminals, scientific instruments blood analyzers, credit card verification, pinball machines, automotive ignition control, and inventory control systems. Industry is using microcomputers and microprocessors in microwave ovens, sewing machines, flow meters, gas station pumps, paint mixing machines, process monitoring, polution monitoring and as control units for hundreds of other devices.

microcomputer chip A microcomputer on a chip. Differs from a microprocessor in that it not only contains the

A self-service banking machine connected to the bank's computer permits customers to transact their banking business at any hour of the day or night. The above unit can be installed in an exterior bank wall, in the bank's lobby, or in remote locations such as shopping centers or airports.

central processing unit (CPU), but also includes on the same piece of silicon a RAM, a ROM and input/outut circuitry. Often called a "computer on a chip." See *microcomputer* and *microprocessor*.

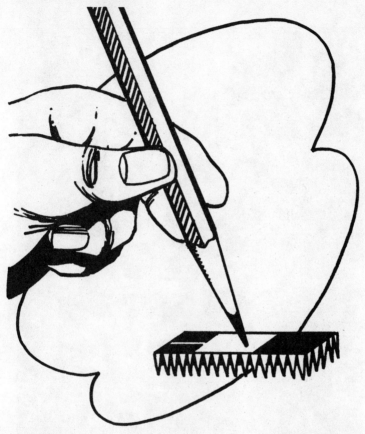

The pencil points to the "computer-on-a-chip," which makes small computers possible.

microcomputer components   The major components of a microcomputer are a microprocessor, a memory (ROM, PROM, EPROM, RAM), and Input/Output circuitry.

microcomputer development system   A computer system, based upon a particular microprocessor, that is utilized for developing both hardware and software. The system usually includes an assembler, text editor, monitor, system console, PROM programmer, and disk/tape system.

Point-of-sale terminals are being used in many department stores to expand and speed sales floor service to customers. In a typical sale, for example, a salesperson merely passes a hand-held wand over the thin magnetic strip on a price tag, without removing it from the merchandise. The terminal then can read, record and print information describing the item, display the price on a lighted panel, compute the amount due including applicable taxes, calculate change to be returned, and print a cash receipt.

microcomputer storage The following types of memory are used for microcomputer instruction and data storage: ROM (Read Only Memory), PROM (Programmable ROM), EPROM (Erasable PROM), and RAM (Random Access Memory).

Detectives in the Norfolk (Virginia) police department use a computer-fingerprint expert to help them solve burglary and auto theft cases. The computer, which contains thousands of coded fingerprints in its memory, is used to rapidly match a thief's fingerprint with a known print in its memory.

microcontroller A device or instrument that controls a process with high resolution, usually over a narrow region. A microprogrammed machine (microcomputer or microprocessor) used in a control operation, that is, to direct or make changes in a process or operation. For example, Singer Company uses a microcontroller and a ROM to operate sewing machines. See *microcomputer* and *microprocessor*.

microfiche A sheet of film about 10.2 cm by 15.2 cm (4 inches by 6 inches) upon which the images of computer output may be recorded. Up to 270 pages of output may be recorded on one sheet of microfiche. See *ultrafiche*.

microfilm Photographic film used for recording graphic information in a reduced size.

microelectronics The field which deals with techniques for producing miniature circuits — for example, integrated circuits, thin film techniques, and solid logic modules.

Industry is making increasing use of computerized systems in all productions. Here a computer reduces overhead at an asphalt and ready mix concrete plant by automating mixing/loading product and maintaining customer records. The computer stores customer mix formulations, apportions batches of material among truckloads, allocates various materials from storage bins into pug mill (mixers) by weight, controls loading and weighing of trucks, prints detailed load tickets, and accumulates customer inventory totals of products.

micrographics The use of miniature photography to condense, store, and retrieve graphic information. Involves the usage of all types of microforms and microimages, such as *microfilm, microfiche,* and *computer output microfilm.*

micrologic The use of a permanent stored program to interpret instructions in a microprogram.

microminiaturization A term implying very small size, one step smaller than miniaturization.

microprocessor An LSI (large scale integration) central processing unit (CPU) on one — or a few — MOS (metal oxide semiconductor) or bipolar chips. Along with arithmetic functions, the CPU may perform input/output jobs and may contain a scratch pad or other memory. To form a working system, at least one external ROM, RAM, or other memory device is usually used with the CPU. Microprocessors are used in microcomputers, computer kits, microwave ovens, phototypesetting machines, automobile electrical systems, automatic gas station pumps, and many other devices. See *microcomputer* and *microcomputer chip.*

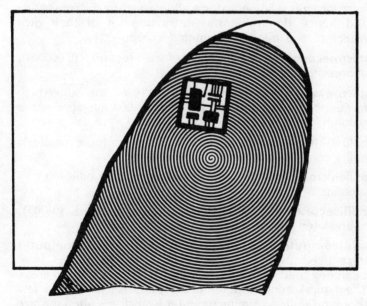

A microprocessor is a semiconductor chip which contains the electronic circuitry necessary for digital arithmetic and logical operations.

**ARITHMETIC/LOGIC UNIT
TIMING AND CONTROL UNIT
GENERAL PURPOSE REGISTERS
ACCUMULATOR AND PROGRAM COUNTER
INSTRUCTION REGISTER AND DECODER
PARALLEL DATA AND I/O BUS
SMALL STACK/STACK POINTER**

Functional parts of a microprocessor.

microprogrammed computer A term referring to any computer whose instruction set is not fixed but can be tailored to individual needs by the programming of ROMs or other memory devices. Consequently whether the computer is a large scale machine, minicomputer or microprocessor — theoretically it can be microprogrammed. See *microprogramming*.

microprogramming A method of operating the control part of a computer where each instruction is broken into several small steps (microsteps) that form part of a microprogram. Some systems allow users to microprogram and hence determine the instruction set of their own machine. See *microprogrammed computer*.

microsecond One-millionth of a second (0.000001); abbreviated μs or μsec.

microwave An electromagnetic wave in the super-high frequency radio spectrum (890 to 300 000 megacycles per second).

milli One-thousandth, used as a prefix; for example, a millisecond is a thousandth of a second.

millimicrosecond Same as nanosecond, one billionth of a second.

millisecond One-thousandth of a second (0.001); abbreviated ms or msec.

minicomputers A relatively inexpensive computer introduced during the mid-1960's. Minicomputers have been designed for use in a wide variety of application areas. The typical minicomputer has a purchase price of a few thousand dollars. A minicomputer is small — often the size of a small suitcase. It is built for simple installation and does not require a closely controlled environment. It can be maintained by the user, and if it is provided with a user oriented software system, it can be programmed and operated by people who are not computer experts. A minicomputer weighs about 80 pounds.

Rapid availability of detailed information and the ability to electronically search comprehensive data files are the keys to the control of crime. Shown here are Little Rock, Arkansas policemen operating a computerized criminal information center.

minuend A number from which another number, called the subtrahend, is to be subtracted. In the subtraction 7–3 = 4, 7 is the minuend, 3 is the subtrahend, and 4 is the difference.

MIS An acronym for *Management Information System.*

mistake A human failing that produces an unintended result; e.g., faulty arithmetic, using incorrect computer instructions, incorrect keypunching, or use of incorrect formula. Contrast with *error, fault,* and *malfunction.* See *bug.*

mixed number A number having a fractional part; e.g., 63.71, –18.006, 298.413.

mnemonic Pertaining to a technique used to aid human memory. A word or name which is easy to remember and identify.

mnemonic code An easy-to-remember assembly language code, for example, a code that uses an abbreviation such as MPY for "multiply."

mnemonic language A programming language that is based on easily remembered symbols and that can be assembled into machine language by the computer.

mode (1) A method of operation. (2) The form of a number, name, or expression.

model See *mathematical model.*

modem An acronym for MOdulator-DEModulator. A device that provides the appropriate interface between a communications link and a data processing machine or system by serving as a modulator and/or demodulator. Same as *data set.*

modify (1) To alter a portion of an instruction so that its interpretation and execution will be other than normal. The modification may permanently change the instruction or leave it unchanged and affect only the current execution. (2) To alter a program according to a defined parameter.

modular programming A technique for designing a system or program as a number of self-contained modules. See *module.*

modulation In data communications, the process by which some characteristic of a high frequency carrier signal is varied in accordance with another, a lower frequency "information" signal. This technique is used in data sets to make computer terminal signals compatible with communication facilities.

modulator A device that receives electrical pulses, or bits, from a data processing machine and converts them into signals suitable for transmission over a communications link. Contrast with *demodulator.*

module (1) Specifically, one logical part of a program. A major program may be broken down into a number of logically self-contained modules. These modules may be written (and tested separately, possibly by a number of programmers). The modules can then be put together to form the complete program. This is called *modular programming.* (2) An interchangeable plug-in item containing components.

modulo A mathematical operator which yields the remainder function of division. Thus 53 modulo 7 is 4.

monitor A control program. See *operating system.*

monolithic integrated circuit A class of integrated circuits wherein the substrate is an active material such as the semiconductor silicon. See *integrated circuit.*

monte carlo A trial and error method of repeated calculations to discover the best solution of a problem. Often used when a great number of variables are present, with interrelationships so extremely complex as to eliminate straightforward analytical handling.

MOS An acronym for *Metallic Oxide Semiconductor.*

MOSFET An acronym for Metallic Oxide Semiconductor Field Effect Transistor. When a voltage (negative with respect to the substrate) is applied to the gate, then the MOSFET is a conductor; and, if a potential difference is applied between source and drain, there will be current flow.

At this international petroleum company's research and development center, two computers are used by engineers for applications involving worldwide oil exploration and petroleum product evaluation and analysis.

MOS/LSI See *metallic oxide semiconductor* and *large scale integration.*

most significant digit Pertaining to the digit of a number that has the greatest weight or significance; e.g., in the number 54321, the most significant digit is 5. Abbreviated MSD. See *high order* and *justify.*

motherboard An interconnecting assembly into which printed circuit cards, or boards, or modules are connected.

move To transfer from one location of storage to another location.

moveable-head disk unit A storage device or system consisting of magnetically coated disks, on the surface of which data is stored in the form of magnetic spots arranged in a manner to represent binary data. These data are arranged in circular tracks around the disks and are accessible to reading and writing heads on an arm which can be moved mechanically to the desired disk and then to the desired track on that disk. Data from a given track are read or written sequentially as the disk rotates.

ms An abbreviation for millisecond.

MSD An acronym for Most Significant Digit.

MSI An acronym for *Medium Scale Integration.*

MTBF An acronym for Mean Time Between Failure. Average length of time a system or component is expected to work without failure.

MTTF An acronym for Mean Time To Failure. The average length of time for which the system, or a component of the system, works without fault.

MTTR An acronym for Mean Time To Repair. Average time expected to be required to detect and correct a fault in a computer system.

multiaddress Pertaining to an instruction format containing more than one address part.

multicomputer system A computer system consisting of two or more central processing units.

multifile sorting The automatic sequencing of more than one file, based upon separate parameters for each file, without operator intervention.

multijob operation A term that describes concurrent execution of job steps from two or more jobs.

multilevel addressing See *indirect addressing.*

multipass sort A sort program which is designed to sort more data than can be contained within the internal memory of a central computer. Intermediate storage, such as disk, tape, drum, etc. is required.

multiple access A system with a number of on-line communication channels providing concurrent access to the common system.

multiple-address instruction An instruction consisting of an operation code and two or more addresses. Usually specified as a two-address, three-address, or four-address instruction.

multiple-address message A message to be delivered to more than one destination.

multiple connector A connector to indicate the merging of several lines of flow into one line, or the dispersal of one line of flow into several lines.

multiple-job processing Controlling the performance of more than one data processing job at a time.

multiple punching The punching of two or more holes in a card column.

multiplex To interleave or simultaneously transmit two or more messages over a single channel or other comunications facility.

multiplexer A device that makes it possible to transmit two or more messages simultaneously over a single channel or other transmission facility.

multiplexor channel A special type of input/output channel that can transmit data between a computer and a number of simultaneously operating peripheral devices.

multiplicand The quantity which is multiplied by another quantity.

multiplication time The time required to perform a multiplication. For a binary number it will be equal to the total of all the addition times and all the shift time involved in the multiplication.

multiplier The quantity which is used to multiply another quantity.

multiprecision arithmetic A form of arithmetic where two or more computer words are used to represent each number.

multiprocessing The simultaneous execution of two or more sequences of instructions by multiple central processing units under common control. See *multiprogramming*.

multiprocessor A computer network consisting of two or more central processors under a common control.

multiprogramming Running two or more programs at the same time in the same computer. Each program is alloted its own place in memory and its own peripherals, but all share the central processing unit. Made economical by the fact that peripherals are slower than the central processing unit, so most programs spend most of their time waiting for input or output to finish. While one program is waiting, another can use the central processing unit.

multireel sorting The automatic sequencing of a file having more than one input tape, without operator intervention.

multitask operation See *multiprogramming*.

MUX An acronym for multiplexer.

MVT An acronym for Multiprogramming with a Variable number of Tasks; the tasks being programs. Also jokingly called Multiprogramming with a Vast amount of Trouble.

mylar A DuPont trademark for polyester film, often used as a base for magnetically coated or perforated information media.

N

name An alphanumeric term that identifies a program, a control statement, data areas, or a cataloged procedure. Same as *label*.

nand A logical operator having the property that if P is a statement, Q is a statement, . . . then the nand of P, Q, . . . is true if at least one statement is false, false if all statements are true.

nanosecond One-billionth of a second (0.000000001), One-thousand-millionth of a second; abbreviated as ns.

Napier, John (1550-1617) A Scottish aristocrat who made many contributions to mathematics and computing. He invented logarithms, a calculating device known as Napier's bones, and is known for improving the abacus.

Napier's bones A set of numbering rods which are used to multiply, divide, and extract roots. The calculating rods were developed by John Napier in 1614 and were used by William Oughtred in 1630 in the invention of the slide rule.

National Computer Conference An annual meeting of computer users and computer equipment manufacturers.

native language A computer language that is peculiar to the machines of one manufacturer.

natural language A human language such as English, German, Spanish, French, etc. Contrast with *artificial language*.

NBS An acronym for National Bureau of Standards. A government agency.

N/C An acronym for Numerical Control.

NCC An acronym for National Computer Conference.

negate To perform the logical operator "NOT."

NELIAC An acronym for Naval Electronics Laboratory International Algorithmic Compiler. A higher level programming language used primarily for solving scientific and real-time control problems.

nesting (1) Including a routine or block of data within a larger routine or block of data. (2) A loop of instructions which may contain another loop and so on perhaps down through several levels.

network The interconnection of a number of points by data communication facilities. See *computer network*.

Newton-Raphson A term applied to an iterative procedure used for solving equations. See *iterate*.

nibble One half of a byte, namely a four-bit data element.

nine's complement A numeral used to represent the negative of a given value. A nine's complement numeral is obtained by subtracting each digit from a numeral containing all nines; for example, 567 is the nine's complement of 432 and is obtained by subtracting 432 from 999.

ninety column card A punched card used with early UNIVAC card handling equipment.

ninety-six column card A punched card used with some card handling equipment. The card physically contains 18 rows and 36 columns as three characters are punched in each column.

NMOS An acronym for N-channel MOS. Circuits that use currents made up of negative charges and produce devices at least twice as fast as PMOS.

noise Loosely, any disturbance tending to interfere with the normal operation of a device or system, including those attributable to equipment components, natural disturbance, or manual interference.

non-destructive read A read operation that does not alter the information content of the storage media.

non-erasable storage A storage device whose information cannot be erased during the course of computation — for example, punched-paper tape, punched cards, and certain non-destructible readout magnetic memories.

nonexecutable A program statement that sets up a program but does not call for any specific action on the part of the program in which it appears. Contrast with *executable*.

nonprint An impulse that inhibits line printing under machine control.

non-sequential computer A computer that must be directed to the location of each instruction.

nonvolatile storage A storage media which retains its data in the absence of power.

no-op An abbreviation of the term *no-operation*.

no-operation instruction A computer instruction whose only effect is to advance the instruction counter. It accomplishes nothing more than the movement beyond itself to the next instruction in normal sequence.

nor The Boolean operator which gives a truth table value of true only when both of the variables connected by the logical operator are false.

normalize To adjust the exponent and fraction of a floating point quantity so that the fraction is within a prescribed range. Loosely, to *scale*.

NOT A logic operator having the property that if P is a statement, then the NOT of P is true if P is false, false if P is true.

notation See *positional notation.*

ns An abbreviation for nanosecond; one-billionth of a second.

nucleus That portion of the control program that must always be present in internal storage.

null An absence of information, as contrasted with zero or blank for the presence of no-information.

number (1) A symbol or symbols representing a value in a specific numeral system. (2) Loosely, a *numeral.*

number base See *radix.*

number crunching A term applied to a program or computer which is designed to perform large amounts of computation and other numerical manipulations of data.

number representation The representation of numbers by agreed sets of symbols according to agreed rules.

number system An agreed set of symbols and rules for number representation. Loosely, a *numeral system.*

numeral A conventional symbol representing a number; e.g., six, 6, VI, 110 are four different numerals that represent the same number.

numeral system A method of representing numbers. In computing, several numeral systems are of particular interest, in addition to the common decimal system. These are the binary, hexadecimal, and octal systems. In each system the value of a numeral is the value of the digits multiplied by the numeral system radix, raised to a power indicated by the position of the digits in the numeral.

numeralization Representation of alphabetic data through the use of digits.

numerator In the expression A/B, A is the numerator and B is the denominator.

numeric Pertaining to numerals or to representation by means of numerals.

numeric character Same as a digit.

numeric coding Coding which uses digits only to represent data and instructions.

numeric data Consist solely of the digits 0-9.

numeric punch A punch in any of rows 1 through 9 of a punch card.

numerical analysis The branch of mathematics concerned with the study and development of effective procedures for computing answers to problems.

numerical control A means of controlling machine tools through servo-mechanisms and control circuitry, so that the motions of the tool will respond to digital coded instructions on tape or to direct commands from a computer. See *APT* and *parts programmer.*

O

obey The process whereby a computer carries out an operation as specified by one or more of the instructions forming the program which is currently being executed.

object code Output from a compiler or assembler which is itself executable machine code or is suitable for processing to produce executable machine code.

object computer A computer used for the execution of an object program.

object deck A set of punched cards representing the machine language equivalent of a source deck.

object language The output of a translation process. Usually object language and machine language are the same. Contrast with *source language.* Synonymous with *target language.*

object language programming Programming in a machine language executable on a particular computer.

object program The instructions which come out of the *compiler* or *assembler,* ready to run on the computer. The object program is the one which is actually run with your data to produce results.

objective The ends toward which an organization works.

OCR An acronym for Optical character Recognition. Characters printed in a special type style which can be read by both machines and people. See *optical character recognition.*

octal Pertaining to a number system with a radix of eight. Octal numbers are frequently used to represent binary numerals, with each octal digit representing a group of three binary digits (bits); e.g., the binary numeral 111000010001101 can be represented as octal 70215.

octal numeral A numeral of one or more digits, representing a sum in which the quantity represented by each figure is based on a radix of eight. The digits used in octal numerals are 0,1,2,3,4,5,6, and 7.

octal point The radix point in an octal numeral system. The point that separates the integer part of a mixed octal numeral from the fractional part. In the numeral 34.17, the octal point is between the digits 4 and 1.

OEM An acronym for Original Equipment Manufacturer. A company or organization that purchases computers and peripheral equipment for use as components in products and equipment that they subsequently sell to their customers.

off-line A term describing equipment, devices, or persons not in direct communication with the central processing unit of a computer. Equipment which are not connected to the computer. Contrast with *on-line*.

off-line storage Storage not under control of the central processing unit.

offset The difference between the value or condition desired and that actually attained.

one-address A computer that employs only one address in its instruction format; e.g., ADD X, where X represents the address in the instruction.

one-address instruction An instruction consisting of an operation and exactly one address. The instruction code of a single address computer may include both zero and multi address instructions as special cases. Most present day computers are of the one-address instruction type. See *one-address computer*.

one-dimensional array An array consisting of a single row or column of elements.

one-for-one A phrase often associated with an assembler where one source language statement is converted to one machine language instruction.

one-out-of-ten code In this code a decimal digit is represented by ten binary digits where only one of the binary digits is permitted to be a 1.

one's complement A numeral used to represent the negative of a given value. A one's complement of a binary numeral is obtained by alternating the bit configuration of each bit in the numeral; for example, 01100101 is the one's complement of the binary numeral 10011010.

on-line A term describing equipment, devices, and persons that are in direct communication with the central processing unit of a computer. Equipment which are physically connected to the computer. Contrast with *off-line.*

on-line problem solving A teleprocessing application in which a number of users at remote terminals can concurrently use a computing system in solving problems on-line. Often, in this type of application, a dialogue or conversation is carried on between a user at a remote terminal and a program within the central computer system.

on-line processing Data processing involving direct entry of data into the computer or direct transmission of output from the computer.

on-line storage Storage under control of the central processing unit.

op A contraction for the term "operation."

op-code See *operation code.*

open ended Having the capability by which the addition of new programs, instructions, subroutines, modifications, terms, or classifications does not disturb the original system.

open shop A computer installation at which computer operation can be performed by a qualified person. Contrast with *closed shop.*

open subroutine A subroutine that is inserted into a routine at each place it is used. Contrast with *closed subroutine.*

operand The data unit or equipment item that is operated upon. An operand is usually identified by an address in an instruction. For example, in "ADD 100 TO 400," 100 and 400 are operands. See *operation code.*

operating ratio See *availability.*

operating system An organized collection of software that controls the overall operations of a computer. The operating system does many basic operations which were performed by hardware in older machines, or which are common to many programs. It is available to the computer at all times either being held in internal storage or on an auxiliary storage device. See *executive, monitor* and *supervisory system.*

operation A defined action. The action specified by a single computer instruction or higher level language statement.

operation center A physical area containing the human and equipment resources needed to process data through a computer and produce desired output. Same as *data processing center.*

operation code The instruction code used to specify the operations a computer is to perform. For example, in "ADD 100 TO 400," "ADD" is the operation code. See *operand.*

operations analysis Same as *operations research.*

operations research A mathematical science devoted to carrying out complicated operations with the maximum possible efficiency. Among the common scientific techniques in operations research are the following: linear programming, probability theory, information theory, game theory, monte carlo method, and queuing theory.

operator (1) In the description of a process, that which indicates the action to be performed on operands. (2) A person who operates a machine. See *computer operator* and *keypunching.*

optical character reader An input device that accepts a printed document as input. It identifies characters by their shapes. See *OCR* and *optical character recognition.*

optical character recognition The recognition of printed characters through the use of eight-sensitive optical machines. See *OCR* and *optical reader.*

optical mark reader An input device that reads graphite marks on cards or pages. See *mark sensing.*

optical printer See *electrostatic printer.*

optical reader See *optical character reader* and *optical mark reader.*

optical scanner See *optical character reader.*

optical scanning See *optical character recognition.*

optimize To select storage addresses which will result in a minimization or maximization of some desired characteristic.

optimum Best and most desirable in view of established criteria.

optimum programming Programming in order to maximize efficiency with respect to some criterion; for example, least storage usage, least usage of peripheral equipment, or least computing time.

optimum tree search A tree search whose object is to find the best of many alternatives.

OR See *exclusive OR* and *inclusive OR*.

OR circuit See *OR-gate*.

order (1) To arrange items according to any specified set of rules. (2) An arrangement of items according to any specified set of rules.

OR-gate A computer circuit containing two switches whose output is a binary one if either or both of the inputs are one. This electrical circuit implements the OR operator.

origin In coding, the absolute memory address of the first location of a program or program segment.

OS An acronym for *Operating System*.

oscillography The projection of a pattern of electrical signals on the face of a cathode ray tube.

oscilloscope A device for displaying on a cathode ray tube screen the value of a voltage versus time; used by computer maintenance technicians.

output (1) Data transferred from a computer's internal storage unit to some storage or output device. (2) The final result of data processing; data that has been processed by the computer. Contrast with *input*.

output area An area of storage reserved for output data. Contrast with *input area*.

output data Data to be delivered from a device or program, usually after some processing. Synonymous with *output*. Contrast with *input data*.

output device A unit used for taking out data values from a computer and presenting them in the desired form to the user. Contrast with *input device*.

overflow In an arithmetic operation, the generation of a quantity beyond the capacity of the register or storage location which is to receive the result.

overhead A collective term for the factors which cause the performance of a program or device to be lower than it would be in the ideal case.

overlap To do something at the same time that something else is being done; e.g., to perform an input operation while instructions are being executed by the central processing unit.

overlay To transfer segments of program from auxiliary storage into internal storage for execution, so that two or more segments occupy the same storage locations at different times. See *page*.

overpunch To add holes in a card column that already contains one or more holes.

P

pack To store several short units of data into a single storage cell in such a way that the individual units can later be recovered; e.g., to store two 4-bit BCD digits in one 8-bit storage location. Opposite of *unpack*.

packing density See *recording density*.

padding A technique used to fill out a fixed-length block of information with dummy characters, items, words, or records.

page A segment of a program or data, usually of fixed length, that has a fixed virtual address but can in fact reside in any region of the computer's internal storage. See *virtual storage*.

page frame A location in the real storage of the computer that can store one page (which usually consists of either 2 or 4K words) of commands or data.

page printer A printer in which an entire page of characters is composed and determined within the device prior to printing.

paging A technique for expanding internal storage capacity in which programs are divided into fixed size segments or pages, and those pages not immediately needed are kept in auxiliary storage.

panel See *control panel* and *plugboard.*

paper tape A continuous strip of paper in which holes are punched to record numerical and alphanumerical information for computer processing. Example: 8-track paper tape is 2.54 cm (1 inch) wide and a character is recorded by punching a code of up to eight holes across the width of tape.

paper tape code The system of coding which is used to relate the patterns of holes in paper tape to the alphanumeric characters they represent.

paper tape punch A code-sensitive output device that translates computer code into an external code on paper tape.

paper tape reader An input device used for translating the holes in a perforated paper roll into machine processable form.

parallel Handling all the elements of a word or message simultaneously. Contrast with *serial.*

parallel access The process of obtaining information from or placing information into storage where the time required for such access is dependent on the simultaneous transfer of all elements of a word from a given storage location.

parallel adder An adder which performs its operations by bringing in all digits simultaneously from each of the quantities involved.

parallel computer A computer in which the digits or data lines are processed concurrently by separate units of the computer.

parallel conversion System of changing to a new data processing system that involves running both the old and new systems simultaneously for a period of time.

parallel operation The performance of several actions, usually of a similar nature, simultaneously through provision of individual, similar or identical devices for each such action. Contrast with *serial operation.*

parallel printing An entire row is printed at one time.

parallel processing Pertaining to the concurrent or simultaneous execution of two or more processes in multiple devices such as processing units or channels. Contrast with *serial processing*.

parallel reading Row-by-row reading of a data card.

parallel transmission In data communications, a method of data transfer in which all bits of a character are set simultaneously. Contrast with *serial transmission*.

parameter An arbitrary constant. A variable in an algebraic expression that temporarily assumes the properties of a constant. For example, in $y = mx+b$, m and b are parameters if either is treated as a constant in a family of lines.

parentheses A grouping symbol ( ).

parity bit An extra bit added to a byte, character, or word, to ensure that there is always either an even number or an odd number of bits, according to the logic of the system. If, through a hardware failure, a bit should be lost, its loss can be detected by checking the parity. The same bit pattern remains as long as the contents of the byte, character, or word remain unchanged. See *parity checking*.

parity checking Automatic error detection by using checking bits along with the numerical bits. See *parity bit*.

partitioning Subdividing one large block into smaller subunits which can be handled more conveniently.

parts programmer A programmer who translates the physical explanation for machining a part into a series of mathematical steps, and then codes the computer instructions for those steps. See *APT* and *numerical control*.

Pascal, Blaise (1623-1662) A French mathematician who built the first desk-calculator type of adding machine in 1642. This device represented the numbers from 0 to 9 with teeth on gears. The machine could perform addition and subtraction.

pass A complete input, processing, and output cycle in the execution of a computer program.

password See *lock code*.

patch (1) A section of coding that is inserted into a program to correct a mistake or to alter the program. (2) A temporary electrical connection.

patching (1) A makeshift technique for modifying a program or correcting programming errors by changing the object code of the program, usually to avoid recompiling or reassembling the program. (2) Making temporary patches to hardware.

path   See *channel.*

pattern recognition   The recognition of forms, shapes, or configurations by automatic means.

PC   An acronym for Program Counter.

PCM   An acronym for Punched Card Machines.

PDP   A designation for computers manufactured by Digital Equipment Corporation, e.g, PDP-8, PDP-10, PDP-11, etc.

perforator   A keyboard device for punching paper tape.

peripheral equipment   The input/output units and auxiliary storage units of a computer system. The units are attached by cables to the central processing unit. Used to get data in, data out, and act as a reservoir for large amounts of data which cannot be held in the central processing unit at one time. The card reader, typewriter, and disk storage unit are all peripherals.

peripheral storage   See *auxiliary storage.*

personal computer   A small low cost (less than $1000) microcomputer introduced during the mid-1970's. Many vendors who sell personal computers also offer them in kit form. Sometimes called home computer. See *computer kit* and *microcomputer.*

PERT   An acronym for Program Evaluation and Review Technique. A management technique for control of large-scale, long-term projects, involving analysis of the time frame required for each step in a process and the relationships of the completion of each step to activity in succeeding steps. See *critical path method.*

PET   A popular, low-cost microcomputer   manufactured by Commodore Business Machines, Inc.

photo-optic memory   A memory that uses an optical medium for storage. For example, a laser might be used to record on photographic film.

physical record   The unit of data for input or output; e.g., a punched card, a tape block, a record on a disk. One or more logical records may be contained in one physical record. Contrast with *logical record.*

To facilitate the booking and tracking of cargo and to streamline freight documentation, this international ocean carrier has implemented a sophisticated, on-line, real-time data communications network. In the network, a computer in New York is linked to terminals in several cities in the United States and Canada.

pi The name of the Greek letter π. The symbol denotes the ratio of the circumference of a circle to its diameter,

$$\pi = 3.141\ 592\ 653\ 589\ 793\ 238\ 462\ 643\ \cdot\ \cdot\ \cdot$$

The notation π was introduced in the eighteenth century by English mathematicians.

picosecond One-trillionth of a second (0.000000000001), one-thousandth of a nanosecond; abbreviated psec.

picture-phone A device that permits you to see the person you are calling when making a telephone call.

PL/I A higher level programming language designed to process both scientific and business applications. The PL/I language contains many of the best features of FORTRAN, COBOL, ALGOL and other languages as well as a number of facilities not available in previous languages.

plasma display A peripheral device with a screen upon which information may be displayed.

PLA An acronym for Programmable Logic Array. An alternative to ROM (Read Only Memory) that uses a standard logic network programmed to perform a specific function. PLAs are implemented in either MOS or bipolar circuits.

platem A backing, commonly cylindrical, against which printing mechanisms strike to produce an impression.

PLATO An acronym for Programmed Logic for Automatic Teaching Operations. A computer-based instructional system that uses large computers and plasma display terminals. The system contains thousands of lessons representing 65 fields of study for all levels, from kindergarten through graduate school. See *computer assisted instruction* and *plasma display.*

PL/M A programming language used to program microcomputers. The language, developed by Intel Corp., is a high-level language that can fully command the microcomputer to produce efficient run-time object code. PL/M was designed as a tool to help microcomputer programmers concentrate more on their problem or application and less on the actual task of programming. PL/M is derived from PL/I, a general purpose programming language.

PL/M Plus An extended version of PL/M developed by National Semiconductor to simplify programming of their microprocessors.

plot To diagram, draw, or map with a *plotter.*

plotter An output unit which graphs data by an automatically controlled pen. Data is normally potted as a series of incremental steps. Primary types of plotters are the drum plotter and the flat-bed plotter. Also called *digital plotter, incremental plotter* and *X-Y plotter.*

plugboard A perforated board used to control the operations of unit record devices. Also called a *control panel.*

PMOS An acronym for P-channel MOS. Refers to the oldest type of MOS circuit where the electrical current is a flow of positive charges.

pointer An address or other indication of location.

point-of-sale terminal A device used in retail establishments to record sales information in a form that can be input directly into a computer. This intelligent terminal is used to capture data in retail stores; i.e., supermarkets or department stores. See *intelligent terminal* and *source data automation*.

POL An acronym for *Procedure-Oriented Language* or *Problem-Oriented Language*.

Polish notation A logical notation for a series of arithmetic operations in which no grouping symbol is used. This notation was developed by a Polish logician, Jan Lukasiewicz in 1929. For example, the expression $Z = A(B+C)$ is represented in Polish notation as $BC+A\times Z$ =, where this expression is read from left to right. Note that the operator follows the operands.

polling In data communications, scanning the networks of terminals or sensors by the computer, asking one after the other if it has any data to submit.

pop Pulling or retrieving data from the top of a program pushdown stack. The stack pointer is decremented to address the last word pushed on the stack. The contents of this location are moved to one of the accumulators or another register. See *push*.

pop instruction A computer instruction which executes the *pop* operation.

port Terminals which provide electrical input and/or output to a circuit or system. The physical communication line between the central processing unit and a peripheral. Each port has a numerical address that the processor uses in communicating through it. Many microprocessors can address up to 256 input and 256 output ports.

portable computer A small microcomputer or minicomputer that can be carried from place to place, i.e., the IBM 5100 portable computer.

POS An acronym for *Point-of-Sale terminal*.

positional notation A method for expressing a quantity, using two or more figures, wherein the successive right to left figures are to be interpreted as coefficients of ascending integer powers of the radix.

post To enter a unit of information on a record.

post edit To edit output data from a previous computation.

post mortem Pertaining to the analysis of an operation after its completion.

post mortem dump A storage dump taken at the end of the execution of a program. See *storage dump*.

147

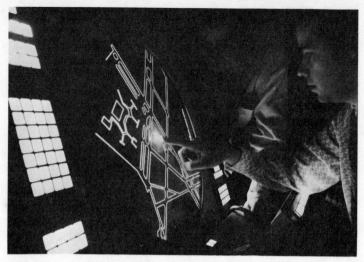

High speed graphic displays that depict computer models of airports, complete with taxiing aircraft, are helping transportation engineers provide answers to aircraft ground control systems of the future. Aircraft are displayed in moving symbols with identification tags that follow an airplane's course on the ground.

power A symbolic representation of the number of times a number is multiplied by itself. The process is called *exponentation*.

power supply kit A typical power supply provides two +18, a + 16, and a − 16 volts. These voltages are unregulated until they reach the individual boards (memory, front panel, etc.). Each board has all the necessary regulation for its own operation. In some kits power supply allows users to expand their computers by adding additional boards inside the main case.

Powers card A ninety column punch card that was used with early UNIVAC card handling equipment.

Powers code A punch card code designed by James Powers for the 1910 census.

pre-canned routines See *canned routines*.

pre-edit See *edit*.

precision The degree of exactness with which a quantity is stated. The result of a calculation may have more precision than it has accuracy; for example, the true value of π to 6 significant digits is 3.14159; the value 3.14162 is precise to 6 digits, given to 6 digits, but is accurate only to about 5. See *accuracy*.

predefined process (1) A process that is identified only by name and that is defined elsewhere. (2) A *closed subroutine*.

predefined process symbol A flowcharting symbol that is used to represent a subroutine.

prefix notation A method of forming mathematical expressions in which each operator precedes its operands; e.g., in prefix notation, the expression "X plus Y multiplied by Z" would be represented by "+XY×Z."

preset To establish an initial condition, such as the control values of a loop or the initial values in index registers. See *initialize*.

preventive maintenance The process used in a computer system which attempts to keep equipment in continuous operating condition by detecting, isolating, and correcting failures before occurrence. It involves cleaning and adjusting the equipment as well as testing the equipment under both normal and marginal conditions. See *corrective maintenance*.

primary storage See *internal storage*.

prime shift A working shift which coincides with the normal business hours of an organization.

print control character A control character for operations on a line printer; e.g., carriage return, page ejection or line spacing.

print wheel A single element providing the character set at one printing position of a wheel printer.

printed circuit An electronic circuit printed, vacuum deposited, or electroplated on a flat insulating sheet.

printer See *electrostatic printer* and *line printer*.

priority processing The processing of a sequence of jobs on the basis of assigned priorities. See *job queue*.

printout See *hard-copy*.

privileged instruction A computer instruction that is not available for use in ordinary programs written by users; its use is restricted to the routines of the operating system. See *storage key* and *storage protection*.

probabilistic model A model that makes use of the mathematics of probability, used to analyze data whose individual values are unknown but whose long-range behavior can be predicted.

probability theory A measure or likelihood of occurrence of a chance event, used to predict behavior of a group.

problem definition The formulation of the logic used to define a problem. A description of a task to be performed.

problem-oriented language A programming language designed for the convenient expression of a given class of problems. See *APT, COGO, GPSS* and *RPG*. Contrast with *assembly language, machine language* and *procedure-oriented language*.

procedure The course of action taken for the solution of a problem. See *algorithm*.

procedure-oriented language A higher level machine-independent, programming language designed for the convenient expression of procedures used in the solution of a wide class of problems. Examples include FORTRAN, COBOL, and PL/I. Contrast with *assembly language, machine langauge* and *problem-oriented language*.

process A systematic sequence of operations to produce a specified result.

process bound Term applied to those programs that generate little input or output, are seldom waiting for data, and therefore result in little central processing unit wait time.

process control The use of the computer to control industrial processes, such as oil refining, and steel production.

process control computer A digital computer used in a process control system. Process control computers are generally limited in instruction capacity, word length, and accuracy. They are designed for continuous operation in non-airconditioned facilities.

process conversion Changing the method of running the computer system.

processing The computer manipulation of data in solving a problem. See *data processing*.

processing symbol A flowcharting symbol used to indicate a processing operation; e.g., a calculation. A rectangular shaped figure is used to represent this symbol.

processor A device or system capable of performing operations upon data; e.g., central processing unit (hardware) or compiler (software). A compiler is sometimes referred to as a language processor.

product The quantity which results from multiplying two quantities.

production run The execution of a debugged program which routinely accomplishes the purpose of the program. For example, running a payroll program to produce weekly paychecks is a production run.

productivity A measure of the work performed by a software/hardware system. Productivity largely depends on a combination of two factors; the facility (ease of use) of the system and the performance (throughout, response time, and availability) of the system.

program (1) A set of sequenced instructions to cause a computer to perform particular operations. (2) A plan to achieve a problem solution. (3) To design, write, and test one or more routines. (4) Loosely, a routine.

program card A card which is punched with specific coding and is used to control the automatic operations of keypunch and verifier machines.

program control Descriptive of a system in which a computer is used to direct the operation of the system.

program deck A set of punched cards containing instructions that make up a computer program.

program flowchart See *flowchart.*

program generator See *generator.*

program language See *programming language.*

program library A collection of available computer programs and routines. Same as *library.* See *disk library* and *tape library.*

program listing See *listing.*

program specifications A document which identifies the data requirements of a system, files required, input-output specifications, and the processing details.

program stack An area of computer memory set aside for temporary storage of data and instructions, particularly during an interrupt. See *pushdown list, push, pushdown stack, pop,* and *stack.*

151

program stop A stop instruction built into the program that will automatically stop the machine under certain conditions, or upon reaching the end of the processing, or completing the solution of a problem.

program storage A portion of the internal storage reserved for the storage of programs, routines and subroutines. In many systems, protection devices are used to prevent inadvertent alteration of the contents of the program storage.

program switch A point in a programming routine at which two courses of action are possible, the correct one being determined by a condition prevailing elsewhere in the program or by a physical disposition of the system.

program testing Executing a program with test data to ascertain that it functions as expected.

programmed check A check consisting of tests inserted into the programmed statement of a problem, and performed by use of computer instructions.

programmer A person whose job it is to design, write, and test programs, the instructions which get the computer to do a specific job. Also called *computer programmer*. See *parts programmer* and *coder*.

programming The process of translating a problem from its physical environment to a language that a computer can understand and obey. The process of planning the procedure for solving a problem. This may involve among other things the analysis of the problem, preparation of a flowchart, coding of the problem, establishing input/output formats, establishing testing and checkout procedures, allocation of storage, preparation of documentation, and supervision of the running of the program on a computer.

programming aids Computer programs that aid computer users; e.g., compilers, debugging packages, linkage editors, and mathematical subroutines.

programming analyst A person skilled in the definition of and the development of techniques and computer programs for the solution of a problem. See *programmer* and *systems analyst*.

programming instruction Refers to a sequence of specific instructions; not to be confused with computer programming, for teaching a human being a specific subject. However, several computer programming training courses have devloped using programmed instruction techniques.

programming language A language used to express computer programs.

PROM An acronym for Programmable Read Only Memory. A memory that can be programmed by electrical pulses. Once programmed, it is read only. The PROM chips can be purchased blank and then be programmed by using a special machine (PROM Programmer). Once programmed, this memory behaves the same as the ROM. That is, it can be read as many times as desired but cannot be written into. Some kinds of PROM can be erased and reused - EPROMs or Erasable PROMs. PROMs are a convenient way for users to implement their own tailor-made application programs. See *EPROM* and *ROM*.

PROM burner See *PROM programmer*.

PROM programmer A device used to program PROMs (Programmable Read Only Memories) and reprogram EPROMs (Erasable PROMs) by electrical pulses. Sometimes called a PROM burner.

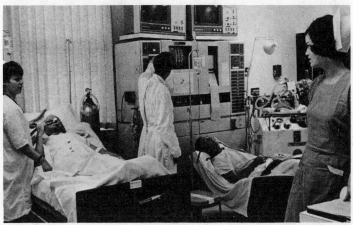

After complicated surgery is performed on a patient, he/she is taken to an intensive care unit. Here many sensors are attached to the patient. These sensors feed data into a computer. The computer monitors these values and alerts medical personnel whenever they enter a danger zone. This automated type of patient monitoring saves the lives of many patients.

protected storage Storage locations reserved for special purposes in which data cannot be stored without undergoing a screening procedure to establish suitability for storage therein.

ps An abbreviation for *picosecond*; one-trillionth of a second.

pseudo code An arbitrary system of symbols used to represent operators, operands, operations, index registers, and so forth.

pseudo language A language, not directly understandable by a computer, which is used to write computer programs. Before a pseudo program can be used, it must be translated into a language that the computer understands (machine language). Same as *symbolic language*.

pseudo operation An operation which is not part of the computer's operation repertoire as realized by hardware; hence an extension of the set of machine operations.

pseudo random number A number generated by a computer in a deterministic manner. These numbers have been subjected to many statistical tests of randomness and for most practical purposes can be used as *random numbers*.

pull instruction An instruction which pulls or retrieves data from the top of the program pushdown stack. Same as *pop instruction*.

pulse modulation Use of a series of pulses, modulated or characterized to convey information. Types of pulse modulation include amplitude (PAM), position (PPM) and duration (PDM) systems.

punched card A cardboard card used in data processing operations in which tiny rectangular holes at hundreds of individual locations denote numerical values, and alphanumeric codes. See *Hollerith card* and *ninety-six column card*.

punched card code A code used to represent data on cards. See *Hollerith code*.

punched paper tape See *paper tape*.

punched tape code See *paper tape code*.

punching position One of the divisions of a card column into which a hole may be punched.

punching station The area on the keypunch and card punch machine where a card is aligned for the punching process.

push Putting data into the top location of a program stack.The stack pointer is automatically incremented to point to the next location which becomes the top of the stack.

push down list A list written from the bottom up, each new entry placed on the top of the list, like a stack of trays in a cafeteria. The item to be processed first is the one on the top of the list - Last In-First Out (LIFO).

push instruction A computer instruction which implements a push operation.

push up list A list of items where each item is entered at the end of the list, and the other items maintain their same relative position in the list.

push down stack A set of memory locations or registers in a computer which implements a pushdown list.

put To place a single data record into an output file.

quality control A technique for evaluating the quality of a product being processed by checking it against a predetermined standard, and taking the proper corrective action if the quality falls below the standard.

quantity A positive or negative real number in the mathematical sense.

quantum The smallest unit of measure employed in a system.

quasi language Same as *pseudo language*.

query To ask for information.

queue A group of items waiting to be acted upon by the computer. The arrangement of items determines the processing priority.

queued access method Any access method that automatically synchronizes the transfer of data between the program using the access method and input/output devices; thereby eliminating delays for input/output operations.

queuing theory A form of probability theory useful in studying delays or lineups at servicing points. Research technique concerned with the correct sequential orders of moving units. May include sequence assignments for bits of information, whole messages, assembly line products, or automobiles in traffic.

quibinary code A binary-coded decimal code for representing decimal numbers in which each decimal digit is represented by seven binary digits.

quotient A result obtained by division.

R

radix The base number in a number system — e.g., the radix in the decimal system is 10. Synonymous with *base*.

radix complement See *complement*.

radix point In a number system, the character (a dot) or implied character that separates the integral part of a numeral from the fractional part; e.g., *binary point, hexadecimal point*, and *octal point*.

radix sorting Same as *digital sorting*.

RAM An acronym for Random Access Memory. (1) A memory chip used with microprocessors. It is the main memory of a microcomputer. Information can be written into and read out of this memory and can be changed at anytime by a new write operation. But the contents are lost when the power is shut off. (2) Random access pertains to the process of obtaining data from or placing data into storage (memory) where the time required for such access is independent of the location of the data most recently obtained or placed in storage.

random access See *direct access*.

random files Files not organized in any sequence. Data are retrieved based on the address of the record on the direct access device.

random number A patternless sequence of digits. An unpredictable number, produced by chance and satisfying one or more of the tests for randomness. See *pseudo random number*.

random number generator A computer program or hardware designed to produce a pseudo-random number or series of pseudo-random numbers according to specified limitations.

rank (1) To arrange in an ascending or descending series according to importance. (2) A measure of the relative position in a group, series, array or classification.

raw data Data which has not been processed.

read To get information from any input or file storage media. For example, reading punched cards by detecting the pattern of holes, or reading a magnetic disk by sensing the patterns of magnetism.

reader Any device capable of transcribing data from an input medium.

reading station The part of a card punch and keypunch where a data card is aligned for reading by a sensing mechanism.

read-only memory See *read-only storage*.

read-only storage A computer storage from which data can be read, but to which no data can be written. Abbreviated *ROM* (read-only memory).

read/write head A small electromagnet used to read, write, or erase data on a magnetic storage device, i.e., disk, tape, drum, magnetic card.

real memory Same as *real storage*.

real storage The internal storage in a virtual memory system.

real time Descriptive of on-line computer processing systems which receive and process data quickly enough to produce output to control, direct, or affect the outcome of an ongoing activity or process. Example — an airline reservation system: a customer booking enquiry is entered into the computer to see if space is available. If a seat is booked, the file of available seats is updated immediately, thus giving an up-to-date record of seats reserved and seats available.

real time clock A piece of hardware which interrupts the processor at fixed time intervals to synchronize the operations of the computer with events occurring in the outside world, often involving human/computer interaction.

real time input Input data inserted into a system at the time of generation by another system.

real time output Output data removed from a system at time of need by another system.

reasonableness check A technique whereby tests are made of processed data to indicate whether a gross error exists. Programming instructions would check if the data lies within pre-set upper and lower limits and initiate some action if the data is not reasonable.

record A collection of related items of data treated as a unit. See *item*.

record gap Same as *interblock gap*.

record layout The arrangement and structure of data in a record, including the size and sequence of its components.

record length A measure of the size of a record, usually specified in units such as words, bytes, or characters.

recording density The number of useful storage cells per unit of length or area; e.g., the number of characters per inch on a magnetic tape, or the number of bits per inch on a single track of a disk. A common recording density for magnetic tape is 1600 characters per inch. Also called *packing density*.

rectifier An electrical device admits current in one direction only.

recursion A set of operations or program statements where one of the operations or statements is specified in terms of the entire set.

recursive Pertaining to a process which is inherently repetitive. The result of each repetition is usually dependent upon the result of the previous repetition.

redundancy check A check based on the transfer of more bits or characters than the minimum number required to express the message itself, the added bits or characters having been inserted systematically for checking purposes. See *parity bit* and *parity checking*.

redundant code A binary coded decimal value with an added check bit.

redundant information A message expressed in such a way that the essence of the information occurs in several ways.

reel A mounting for a roll of tape.

reentrant   Pertaining to a routine that can be used by two or more independent programs at the same time.

reflected code   Same as *gray code*.

refresh   (1) A signal sent to dynamic RAM every few milliseconds to help it remember data. (2) To re-record an image on a cathode ray tube screen when it begins to fade.

regenerate   The process of renewing some quantity. Used in storage devices to write back information that has been read in a destructive manner.

register   A high-speed device used in a central processing unit for temporary storage of small amounts of data or intermittent results during processing.

register pair   In the 8080 microprocessor, a pair of general purpose registers that together make up a 16-bit word that is treated as a unit.

registration   The accurate positioning relative to a reference.

relational expression   An expression which contains one or more relational operators.

relational operator   A symbol used to compare two values; the operator specifies a condition that may be either true or false, such as = (equal to), < (less than), > (greater than), etc.

relative address   An address to which a base address must be added in order to form the absolute address of a particular storage location.

relative coding   Coding that uses machine instructions with relative addresses.

relay   An electromagnetic switching device, having multiple electrical contacts, energized by electrical current through its coil. Used in pre-electronic computers.

reliability   A measure of the ability of a system or individual hardware device to function without failure.

relocatable program   A program existing in a form that permits it to be loaded and executed in any available region of a computer's internal storage.

relocate   To move a program from one area of internal storage to another and, to also adjust the address references so that the program can be executed in its new location.

remainder   The dividend minus the product of the quotient and divisor.

remote access Relating to the communication with a computer facility by a station (or stations) that are distant from the computer.

remote batch processing The processing of data in batches at a remote location, using a small computer system. See *batch processing*.

remote processing The processing of computer programs through an input/output device that is remotely connected to a computer system. See *remote batch processing*.

remote station See *terminal*.

remote terminal A device for communicating with computers from sites which are physically separated from the computer, and often distant enough so that communications facilities such as telephone lines are used rather than direct cables. See *terminals*.

repeating decimal number A nonterminating decimal number such as .3333333 · · · or .31282828 · · ·

reperforator A paper tape punch.

repertoire A complete set of instructions that belongs to a specific computer or family of computers.

repetition instruction An instruction that causes one or more instructions to be executed an indicated number of times.

replacement theory The mathematics of deterioration and failure, used to estimate replacement costs and determine optimum replacement policies.

report Usually associated with output data; involves the grouping of related facts so as to be easily understood by the reader.

report file File generated during data processing, usually used to print out or display desired output.

report generator See *RPG*.

report program generator See *RPG*.

reproduce To copy information on a similar media — for example, to obtain a duplicate disk pack from a specific disk pack.

reproducer Same as *reproducing punch*.

reproducing punch A device for duplicating decks of cards. The reproducing punch is capable of giving an exact copy of a master deck, or a copy of the deck may be punched in a different format.

reprogramming Changing a program written for one computer so that it will run on another.

rerun To repeat all or part of a program on a computer.

reserve accumulator An auxiliary storage register allied to the main accumulator in a central processing unit. See *accumulator.*

reserved words Certain words which, because they are reserved by operating systems, language translators, etc. for their own use, cannot be used in an application program.

reset (1) To return computer components to a specified static state. (2) To place a binary cell into the zero state.

resident program A program that occupies a dedicated area of internal storage.

resource Any facility of the computer system or operating system required by a job or task and including, input/output devices, the central processing unit, internal storage, control and processing programs, and operating personnel.

resource allocation The sharing of computer resources among competing tasks.

resource sharing The sharing of one central processor by both several users and several peripheral devices.

response time The time it takes the computer system to react to a give input. It is the interval between an event and the system's response to the event.

restart To reestablish the execution of a routine.

retrieval See *information retrieval.*

return (1) A set of instructions at the end of a subroutine which permits control to return to the proper point in the main program. (2) A key on an input device that returns the carriage to its leftmost position. See *carriage return.*

reusable The attribute of a routine that permits the same copy of the routine to be used by two or more tasks.

rewind To return a magnetic tape to its starting position on the tape.

right justify See *justify.*

rod memory A computer storage consisting of wires, coated with a nickel-iron alloy, cut in such as way as to form stacks of rods. See *thin-film*.

roll-back A system that will restart the running program after a system failure. Snapshots of data and programs are stored at periodic intervals and the system rolls back to restart at the last recorded snapshot.

roll-out To record the contents of internal storage in auxiliary storage.

ROM An acronym for Read Only Memory. Non-erasable, permanently programmed memory usually used to store monitors, I/O drivers, interpreters, or special application functions. Read Only Memory is very similar to RAM except for one thing. It is not possible to write into ROM memory as it is into RAM. When purchasing a ROM, the user must specify to the manufacturer exactly what is wanted in the memory. Programs stored in ROM are called *firmware*. See *EPROM* and *PROM*.

ROM simulator A general purpose device that is used to replace ROMs or PROMs in a system during program checkout. Because it offers real time in-circuit simulation, it can be used in the engineering prototype or preproduction model to find and correct program errors, or in the production model to add new features.

round See *round-off*.

round-off To truncate the rightmost digit of a number and to increase by one the now remaining rightmost digit if the truncated digit is greater than or equal to half of the number base. For example, the base 10 number 463.1076 would be rounded to 463.108 while the number 23.602 would be rounded to 23.60.

round-off error The error resulting from rounding off a quantity by deleting the less significant digits and applying the same rule of correction to the part retained; for example, 0.2751 can be rounded to 0.275 with a round-off error of .0001. Contrast with *truncation error*.

routine A set of machine instructions for carrying out a specific processing operation. Sometimes used as a synonym for program.

routing The assignment of a path.

row (1) The horizontal members of one line of an array. (2) One of the horizontal lines of punching positions on a punched card. Contrast with *column*.

RPG An acronym for Report Program Generator. A popular business-oriented programming langauge. The language will allow a user to program many business operations as well as generate reports. A fairly simple RPG program can perform a rather sophisticated business task. The langauge is relatively easy to learn.

RPROM An acronym for Reprogrammable PROM. See *EPROM*.

run The single and continuous execution of a program by a computer on a given set of data. Also called *execution*.

run manual A manual or book documenting the processing system, program logic, controls, program changes, and operating instructions associated with a computer run.

run time The time during which the data are fetched by the control unit and the actual processing is performed in the arithmetic unit. Also called *execution time*.

S

SAM An acronym for Sequential Access Method. A method for storing and retrieving data on a disk tile.

sample data A set of hypothetical data used to see if a flowchart is logical and if a program works. See *test data*.

sampling Obtaining a value of a variable at regular or intermittent intervals.

satellite See *communication satellite*.

satellite computer (1) An additional computer, usually smaller, which supports a larger computer system. An economy of processing can be effected if the satellite computer handles lower level functions such as remote terminal coordination, data validity checking, code conversion and input/output functions. (2) An off-line auxiliary computer.

scale A technique used to alter or change the measure of units so that all variables are expressed within a certain range of magnitude.

scale factor One or more factors used to multiply or divide quantities occurring in a problem and convert them into a desired range, such as the range from plus one to minus one.

scan To examine point-by-point in logical sequence.

scanner channel A device which polls individual channels to see if they have data ready to be transmitted.

scatter read-gather write Scatter read refers to placing information from an input record into nonadjacent storage areas. Gather write refers to placing information from nonadjacent storage areas into a single physical record.

SCCS An acronym for Southern California Computer Society. A professional organization of people interested in computers.

scheduling The task of determining what the succession of programs should be in a multiprogramming computer system.

scientific notation A notation in which numbers are written as a "significant digits" part times an appropriate power of 10; e.g., 0.32619×10^7 or $0.32619E+07$ to mean 3 261 900.

SCR An acronym for Silicon Controlled Rectifier, a semiconductor device useful in controlling large amounts of DC current or voltage. Basically it's a diode turned on or off by a signal voltage applied to a control electrode called the *gate*. Its characteristics are similar to the old vacuum tube thyratron, which is why it is sometimes called a thyristor.

scratchpad A small, fast storage that is used in some computers in place of registers.

SCS An acronym for Society for Computer Simulation. A professional computer science organization that is devoted primarily to the advancement of simulation and allied technology.

search To examine a set of items for those that have a desired property.

search key Data to be compared to specified parts of each item for the purpose of conducting a search.

search memory See *associative memory.*

second Base unit of time in the SI metric system, also used in our customary English system.

second generation Computers belonging to the second era of technological development of computers when the transistor replaced the vacuum tube. These were prominent from 1959 to 1964, and were displaced by computers using integrated circuitry.

secondary storage See *auxiliary storage*.

sector One of the peripheral elements into which each track of a disk surface is divided.

security See *computer security* and *data security*.

seed A constant used to initiate a pseudo-random number generator. The seed is used to generate the first number, and all subsequent numbers are based on previous results.

seeks To position the access mechanism of a direct access device at a specified location.

segment (1) To divide a program into parts such that some segments may reside in internal storage and others in auxiliary storage. Each segment will contain the necessary instructions to jump to another segment or to call another segment into internal storage. (2) The smallest functional unit that can be loaded as one logical entity during execution of an overlay program. (3) As applied to telecommunications, a portion of a message that can be contained in a buffer of specified size.

selecting Extracting certain cards from a deck for a specific purpose without disturbing the sequence in which they were originally filed.

selection Choosing between alternative choices.

selector channel A term used in certain computer systems for an input/output channel that can transfer data to or from only one peripheral device at a time. Contrast with *multiplexor channel*.

self-adapting Pertaining to the ability of a system to change its performance characteristics in response to its environment.

self-checking code Same as *error-detection code*.

self-compiling compiler A compiler that is written in its own source language and is capable of compiling itself.

self-complementing code A code which has the property that the binary-one's complement of the weighted binary number is also the numbers-nine's complement in decimal notation.

self-correcting code   A numerical coding system in which transmission errors are automatically detected and corrected. Same as *error-correcting code.*

semantics   The study or science of meaning in language forms.

semi-random access   The method of locating data in storage which combines in the search for the desired item some form of direct access, usually followed by a limited sequential search.

semiconductor   A solid with an electrical conductivity that lies between the high conductivity of metals and the low conductivity of insulators. Semiconductor circuit elements include crystal diodes and transistors.

semiconductor device   An electronic element fabricated from crystalline materials such as silicon or germanium which in the pure state are neither good conductors or good insulators - and unusable for electronic purposes. When certain impurity atoms such as phosphorus or arsenic are diffused into the crystal structure of the pure metal, the electrical neutrality is upset, introducing positive or negative charge carriers. Diodes and transistors can then be implemented.

semiconductor storage   A computer storage whose medium is a semiconductor circuit.

sense   (1) To examine, particularly relative to a criterion. (2) To determine the present arrangment of some element of hardware. (3) To read holes punched on a card or tape.

sense switch   A computer console switch that may be interrogated by a program. Sense switches are very useful when debugging a large, complex program.

sensitivity   The degree of response of a control unit to a change in the incoming signal.

sensors   Devices to detect and measure physical phenomena, such as temperature, stress, heartbeat, wind direction, and fire.

sequence   An arrangement of items according to a specified set of rules.

sequence check   A check used to prove that a set of data is arranged in ascending or descending order.

sequential   Pertaining to the occurrence of events in time sequence, with little or no simultaneity or overlap of events.

sequential computer   A computer in which events occur in time sequence with little or no simultaneity or overlap of events.

sequential file organization   The organization of records in a specific sequence, based on a key such as part number or employee ID. The records in sequential files must be processed one after another.

serial   (1) Pertaining to the sequential occurrence of two or more related activities in a single device. (2) The handling of data in a sequential fashion. Contrast with *parallel*.

serial access   Descriptive of a storage device or medium where there is a sequential relationship between access time and data location in storage — i.e., the access time is dependent upon the location of the data. Contrast with *direct access*. See *serial processing*.

serial adder   An adder that performs its operations by bringing in one digit at a time from each of the quantities involved.

serial computer   A computer in which each digit or data word bit is processed serially by the computer.

serial operation   Computer operation in which all digits of a word are handled sequentially, rather than simultaneously. Contrast with *parallel operation*.

serial processing   Reading, and/or writing, records of file, one by one, in the physical sequence in which they are stored. Contrast with *parallel processing*. See *serial access*.

serial reading   Column-by-column reading of a punch card.

serial transmission   A method of information transfer in which the bits composing a character are sent sequentially. Contrast with *parallel transmission*.

service bureau   An organization which provides data processing service for other individuals or organizations. See *computer utility*.

service programs   See *systems programs*.

servomechanism   Any feedback control system.

set   (1) To place a binary cell into the one state. (2) To place a storage device into a specified state, usually other than denoting zero or blank. (3) A collection.

setup   An arrangement of data or devices to solve a particular problem.

setup time The time between computer runs or other machine operations that is devoted to such tasks as changing disk packs and moving cards, forms, and other supplies to and from the equipment.

shared file A direct access device which may be used by two systems at the same time. A shared file may link two computer systems.

shift To move the characters of a unit of information columnwise right or left. For a number, this is equivalent to multiplying or dividing by a power of the base of notation.

SI Standard abbreviation of the International Metric System, used around the world.

sifting A method of internal sorting where records are moved to permit the insertion of records. Also called *insertion method.*

sign Used in the arithmetic sense to describe whether a number is positive or negative.

sign digit The digit in the sign position of a word.

sign extension The duplication of the sign bit in the higher order positions of a register. This extension is usually performed on one's or two's complement binary values.

sign flag A flip-flop that goes to logic 1 if the most significant bit of the result of an operation has the value, logic 1.

sign position The position at which the sign of a number is located.

signal In communication theory, an intentional disturbance in a communication system. Contrast with *noise.*

signal-to-noise ratio In data communications, the ratio of the (wanted) signal to the (unwanted) noise.

significant digits If the digits of a number are ranked according to their ascending higher-powers of the base, than the significant digits are those ranging from the highest-power digit (different from zero) and ending with the lowest-power digit.

simplex Pertaining to a communications link that is capable of transmitting data in only one direction. Contrast with *full duplex* and *half duplex.*

168

SIMSCRIPT A higher level language specifically designed for programming simulation applications.

simulation To represent the functioning of one system by another; that is, to represent a physical system by the execution of a computer program, or to represent a biological system by a mathematical model. See *mathematical model.*

simulator A device, computer program, or system that represents certain features of the behavior of a physical or abstract system.

simultaneous processing The performance of two or more data processing tasks at the same instant of time. Contrast with *concurrent processing.*

single address See *one-address instruction.*

skip To ignore one or more instructions in a sequence of instructions.

slide rule A device for approximate calculation using the principle of the logarithm.

SLT An acronym for Solid Logic Technique. A term coined by IBM to refer to a microelectronic packaging technique for producing a circuit module.

small business computer A stand alone data processing system, built around a digital computer system, dedicated to the processing of standard business applications — payroll, accounts receivable and payable, order entry, inventory, and general ledger.

small scale integration Early integrated circuit chips.

snapshot dump A dymanic dump of the contents of specified storage locations and/or registers that is performed at specified points or times during the running of a program.

SNOBOL A string manipulation programming language used primarily in language translation, program compilation, and combinatorial problems. The language stresses the ability to manipulate symbolic rather than numeric data.

software A set of programs, procedures, routines, and documents associated with the operation of a computer system. Software is the name given to the programs that cause a computer to carry out particular operations. The software for a computer system may be classified as *application programs* and *systems programs*. Contrast with *hardware*.

software resources The program and data resources that represent the software associated with a computing system.

solid-state Descriptive of electronic components whose operation depends on the control of electric or magnetic phenomena in solids, such as integrated circuits, and transistors.

solid state device A device built primarily from solid state electronic circuit elements.

son file See *father file*.

sort (1) To arrange records according to a logical system. Nowdays, most sorting is done on the computer using magnetic disks, drums, or tapes. (2) A utility program which sorts records held on disk, drum, or tape.

sort generator A program which generates a sort program for production running.

sorter A device that arranges a set of card records in a preselected sequence.

sort/merge program A generalized processing program that can be used to sort or merge records in a prescribed sequence.

SOS An acronym for Silicon On Sapphire. Refers to the layers of material and to the process of fabrication of devices that achieve bipolar speeds through MOS technology by insulating the circuit components from each other. A modern developing semiconductor technology.

source One of three terminal or electrodes of a Field Effect Transistor (FET). The source is the origin of the charge carriers.

source code Symbolic code in its original form before being processed by a computer.

source computer A computer used to translate a source program into an object program.

source data automation The data which is created while an event is taking place is entered directly into the system in a machine processable form. See *point-of-sale terminal*.

source deck A card deck comprising a computer program, in source language.

source document An original document from which basic data is extracted; e.g., invoice, sales slip, inventory tag.

source language The original form in which a program is prepared prior to processing by the computer; e.g., a program written in FORTRAN or assembly language. Contrast with *object language*.

source program A computer program written in a source language such as BASIC, FORTRAN, COBOL, PL/I or assembly language. It is converted to the machine code object program by a special processing program, a compiler or assembler.

source register The register that contains a data word that is being transferred.

SPA An acronym for Systems and Procedures Association. A professional organization whose purpose is to promote advanced management systems and procedures through seminars, professional education, and research.

space One or more blank characters.

special character A graphic character that is neither a letter, a digit, or a blank; e.g., plus sign, equal sign, asterisk, dollar sign, comma, and period.

special-purpose Being applicable to a limited class of uses without essential modification. Contrast with *general-purpose*.

special-purpose computer A computer capable of solving only a few selected types of numerical or logical problems.

specification sheet A form used for coding RPG statements.

spike A sharp peaked, short duration voltage transient.

spooling The process by which various input/output devices appear to be operating simultaneously when actually the system is inputting or outputting data via buffers.

squeezer The person that lays out the LSI circuit in its original "large" form.

SSI An acronym for *Small Scale Integration*.

stack A block of successive storage locations or special registers in a central processing unit, and accessible from one end on a Last In-First Out (LIFO) basis. A stack pointer is incremented by one before each new data item is "pulled" or "popped" from the stack, and decremented by

171

one after a word is "pushed" onto the stack. See *program stack* and *stack pointer*.

stack pointer   A register that is used to point to locations in the stack.

stacked job processing   A technique that permits multiple jobs to be stacked for presentation to the system, which automatically processes the jobs, one after the other. A series of jobs to be executed is placed in a card reader. The computer system executes the jobs automatically in accordance with the job control cards for each job.

stacker   See *card stacker*.

standard   (1) A guide used to establish uniform practices and common techniques. (2) A yardstick (meterstick!) used to measure performance of the computer system function. See *ANS*.

standard interface   A standard physical means by which all peripheral devices are connected to the central processing unit; e.g., a standard form of plug and socket.

standardize   To establish standards or to cause conformity with established standards.

standby equipment   A duplicate set of equipment to be used if the primary unit becomes unusable because of malfunction.

standby time   (1) The period between placing an inquiry into the equipment and the availability of the reply. (2) The period after the set-up of the equipment for use and its actual use. (3) The period during which the equipment is available for use.

state   Used most often to refer to the condition of bistable devices, which are used to represent binary digits. By definition, such devices can have only two states. The state of a switch describes whether it is on or off.

statement   In programming, an expression or generalized instruction in a source language.

static   In storage, information that is fixed at all times.

staticizing   The process of transferring an instruction from computer storage to the instruction registers and holding it there, ready to be executed.

station   One of the input or output points on a data communications system. See *terminal*.

statistics The branch of mathematics that collects information and tabulates and analyzes it.

step (1) To cause a computer to execute one instruction. (2) One instruction in a computer routine.

storage Descriptive of a device or medium that can accept data, hold them, and deliver them on demand at a later time. The term is preferred to memory. Synonymous with memory. See *auxiliary storage, internal storage, PROM, protected storage, RAM* and *ROM*.

storage allocation The assignment of specific programs, program segments, and/or blocks of data to specific portions of a computer's storage. Sometimes called *memory allocation*. See *program storage*.

storage block A contiguous area of internal storage.

storage capacity The number of items of data which a storage device is capable of containing. Frequently defined in terms of computer words, bytes, or characters.

storage device A device used for storing data within a computer system; e.g., integrated circuit storage, magnetic disk unit, magnetic tape unit, magnetic drum unit, floppy disk, tape cassette, etc.

storage dump A printout of all or part of the contents of the internal storage of a computer; used to diagnose errors. Also called *memory dump*. See *post mortem dump* and *snapshot dump*.

storage key An indicator associated with a storage block or blocks, which requires that tasks have a matching protection key to use the blocks. See *privileged instruction* and *storage protection*.

storage location A position in storage where a character, byte, or word may be stored. Same as *cell*.

storage map A diagram that shows where programs and data are stored in the storage units of the computer system.

storage protection Protection against unauthorized writing in and/or reading from all or part of a storage device. Storage protection is usually implemented automatically by hardware facilities, usually in connection with an operating system. Sometimes called *memory protection*. See *storage key*.

storage unit See *storage device*.

store (1) The British term for storage. (2) To place in storage.

store-and-forward In data communications, the process of message handling used in a message-switching system.

stored program computer A computer capable of performing sequences of internally stored instructions and usually capable of modifying those instructions as directed by the instructions. Same as *digital computer.*

stored program concept Instructions to a computer as well as data values are stored within the internal storage of a computer. The instructions can, thus, be accessed more quickly and may be more easily modified. This concept was introduced by John von Neumann in 1945. It is the most important characteristic of the digital computer. See *John von Neumann.*

straight line code The repetition of a sequence of instructions by explicitly writing the instructions for each repetition. Generally straight line coding will require less execution time and more space than equivalent loop coding. The feasibility of straight line coding is limited by the space required as well as the difficulty of coding a variable number of repetitions.

string Data comprised of a string of bits or characters without recognizable field or record boundaries.

string manipulation A technique for manipulating strings of characters.

structured programming A technique for designing and writing computer programs that constructs a program in independent logic or data segments in a hierarchial structure, using a limited number of basic statement types and a minimum of branching to produce programs that can be read from top to bottom. The technique is concerned with improving the programming process through better organization of programs and better programming notation to facilitate correct and clear description of data and control structures.

stub card A card containing a detachable stub to serve as a receipt for future reference.

subprogram Same as *subroutine.*

subroutine A subsidiary routine, within which initial execution never starts. It is executed when called by some other program, usually the main program. Also called *subprogram*. See *closed subroutine* and *open subroutine*.

subroutine reentry Initiation of a subroutine by one program before it has finished its response to another program which called for it. This is what may happen when a control program is subjected to a priority interrupt.

subscript A programming notation that is used to identify an element in an array.

subscripted variable A symbol whose numeric value can change. It is denoted by an array name followed by a subscript; e.g., CHESS(2,4) or A(7). See *subscript* and *variable*.

subset A set contained within a set.

substring A portion of a character string.

subsystem Systems subordinate to the main system.

subtrahend The quantity which is subtracted from another quantity. In the difference A–B, B is the subtrahend and A is the minuend.

sum The quantity which results from adding two quantities.

summarize To condense a mass of data into a concise and meaningful form.

summary punch A card punch operating in conjunction with another machine, usually a tabulator, to punch into cards data which have been summarized or calculated by the other machine.

superscript A letter or digit written above a symbol to denote a power or to identify a particular element of a set; e.g., x^3.

supervisory system See *operating system*.

suppress To eliminate zeros or other insignificant characters from a computer printout.

swapping In virtual storage, occurs when a new page is brought into internal storage from auxiliary storage and swapped for an existing page.

switch See *program switch*.

symbol (1) A letter, numeral or mark which represents a numeral, operation or relation. (2) An element of the computer's character set.

symbol string A string consisting solely of symbols.

symbolic table A mapping for a set of symbols to another set of symbols or numbers; for example, in an assembler, the symbol table contains the symbolic label addresses of an assembled object program.

symbolic address An address expressed in symbols convenient to the program writer, which must be translated into an absolute address (usually by an assembler) before it can be interpreted by a computer.

symbolic coding Coding in which the instructions are written in non-machine language; i.e., coding using symbolic notation for operation codes and operands.

symbolic device A name used to indicate an input/output file; e.g., SYSDSK used to specify the magnetic disk unit.

symbolic language A pseudolanguage made up of letters, characters, and numbers which are not the internal language of the computer system. See *assembly language*, and *higher level language*.

symbolic logic The discipline that treats formal logic by means of a formalized artificial language whose purpose is to avoid the ambiguities and logical inadequacies of natural language.

symbolic name See *name*.

symbolic programming Using a symbolic language to prepare computer programs.

synchronization Adjustment of the chronological relationships between events, either to cause them to coincide, or to maintain a fixed time difference between them.

synchronization check A check that determines whether a particular event or condition occurs at the proper moment.

synchronous computer A computer in which each operation starts as a result of a signal generated by a clock. Contrast with *asynchronous computer*.

synchronous transmission The transmission technqiue that presents data in a continuous flow of pulses. Once synchronization has been established by a special synchronizing pulse, the pattern of pulses received in a given time period is recorded.

synonym Two or more keys that produce the same table address when hashed.

syntax The grammatical and structural rules of a language. All assembly and higher level programming languages possess a formal syntax.

SYSGEN An acronym for SYStems GENeration. The process of modifying the generalized operating system received from the vendor into a tailored system meeting the unique needs of the individual user.

system An organized grouping of people, methods, machines, and materials collected together to accomplish a set of specific objectives. See *computer system*.

system commands Special instructions given to the computer when one operates in the conversational time sharing mode. System commands direct the computer to execute (RUN) programs, list them (LIST), save them (SAVE), and to do other operations of a similar nature.

system flowchart See *flowchart*.

system interrupt A break in the normal execution of a program or routine which is accomplished in such a way that the usual sequence can be resumed from that point later on.

systems analysis The examination of an activity, procedure, method, technique, or a business to determine what must be accomplished and how the necessary operations may best be accomplished by using data processing equipment.

systems analyst One who studies the activities, methods, procedures, and techniques of organizational systems in order to determine what actions need to be taken and how these actions can best be accomplished.

systems programming The development of programs which form operating systems for computers. Such programs include assemblers, compilers, control programs, input/output handlers, etc.

systems manual A document containing information on the operation of a system. Sufficient detail is provided so that management can determine the data flow, forms used, reports generated, and controls exercised. Job descriptions are generally provided.

systems programs Computer programs that provide a particular service to the user; for example, compilers, assemblers, operating systems, sort-merge programs, emulators, linkage editor programs, graphic support programs, and mathematical programs. See *manufacturer's software* and *utility routines*.

systems study An investigation made to determine the feasibility of installing or replacing a business system. See *feasibility study*.

systems synthesis The planning of the procedures for solving a problem.

systems testing Involves the testing of a series of programs in succession, to make sure that all of the programs, their input, and output, are related in the way the system analyst intended.

T

table A collection of data in a form suitable for ready reference, frequently as stored in consecutive storage locations or written in the form of an array of rows and columns for easy entry, and in which an intersection of labeled rows and columns serves to locate a specific piece of data or information.

table look-up A procedure for using a known value to locate an unknown value in a table.

tabulate (1) To print totals. (2) To form data into a table.

tabulating equipment Unit record machines which use punched cards and are predominately electromechanical, such as sorters, collators, interpreters, reproducing punches and tabulators.

tag A portion of an instruction. The tag carries the number of the index register that affects the address in the instruction.

tape A strip of material, which may be punched or coated with a magnetic sensitive substance, and used for data input, storage, or output. The data are usually stored serially in several channels across the tape transversely to the reading or writing motion.

tape cartridge See *magnetic tape cartridge*.

tape cassette See *magnetic tape cassette*.

tape code See *magnetic tape code* and *paper tape code*.

tape deck Same as *magnetic tape unit*.

tape drive Same as *magnetic tape drive*.

tape handler See *magnetic tape unit*.

tape library A special room which houses a file of magnetic tapes under secure, environmentally-controlled conditions.

tape unit See *magnetic tape unit, paper tape punch* and *paper tape unit*.

tape label Usually the first record on a magnetic tape reel, containing such information as the date the tape was written, identification name or number, and the number of records on the tape.

tape-to-card converter A device which converts information directly from paper tape or magnetic tape to punch cards, usually off-line.

target language The language into which some other language is to be properly translated. Usually has the same meaning as *object language*.

target program Same as *object program*.

tariff In data communications, the published rate for a specific unit of equipment, facility or type of service provided by a communication common carrier.

task A unit of work for the computer.

telecommunications The transfer of data from one place to another over communication lines. See *data communications*.

telemetry Transmission of data from remote measuring instruments by electrical or radio means; e.g., data can be telemetered from a space craft circling the moon and recorded at a ground station located on earth.

teleprinter A form of typewriter.

teleprocessing The use of telephone lines to transmit data and commands between remote locations and a data processing center or between two computer systems. Data processing combined with data communications.

teletypewriter A Teletype unit. A generic term referring to teleprinter equipment and to the basic equipment made by the Teletype Corp. A device used widely as an input/output unit to microcomputers and minicomputers, and as a

179

terminal in time sharing computer systems. Abbreviated TTY.

TELEX Western Union's teletypewriter exchange service which allows point-to-point connections using a variety of input/output devices.

Telpak A service offered by communications common carriers for the leasing of wide band channels between two or more points.

template See *flowchart template*.

temporary storage In programming, storage locations reserved for intermediate results. Synonymous with *working storage*.

ten's complement A number used to represent the negative of a given value. A ten's complement number is obtained by subtracting each digit from a number containing all nines and adding one; for example, 654 is the ten's complement of 346 and is obtained by performing the computation 999–346+1.

terminal (1) An input/output peripheral device which is on-line to the computer, but which is in a remote location: another room, another city, or another country. (2) A point at which information can enter or leave a communication network.

terminal symbol A flowcharting symbol used to indicate the starting point and termination point or points in a procedure. An oval shaped figure is used to represent this symbol.

test data Data especially created to test the operation of a given program. Usually, one or more hand-calculated results, or otherwise known results, will be associated with test data so the program under test may be validated.

testing Running a program with sample data, in order to *debug* it. See *systems testing*.

text That part of the message which contains the information to be conveyed.

theory of numbers A branch of pure mathematics concerned generally with the properties and relationships of integers.

thesaurus A lexicon, more especially where words are grouped by ideas; a grouping or classification of synonyms or near synonyms; a set of equivalent classes of terminology.

thin film A computer storage made by placing thin spots of magnetic materials on an insulated base (usually a flat plate or wire); electric current in wires attached to the base is used to magnetize the spot. See *rod memory*.

third generation Computers which use integrated circuitry and miniaturization of components to replace transistors, reduce costs, work faster, and increase reliability. The third generation of computers began in 1964.

thrashing Overhead associated with memory swapping in a virtual memory system. Also called *churning*.

three-address computer A computer that employs three addresses in its instruction format. For example, in the instruction ADD A B C, the values represented by A and B are added and the result is assigned to C.

three-dimensional array An array which provides a threefold classification: row, column, and layer.

throughput The total amount of useful processing carried out by a computer system in a given time period.

TICCIT An acronym for Timeshared, Interactive, Computer-Controlled, Instructional Television. A computer aided instruction system that uses minicomputers and modified color television sets as terminals to provide individual instruction to many students simultaneously. See *computer assisted instruction* and *PLATO*.

tie line A leased communication channel.

time sharing A method of operation in which a computer facility is shared by several users for different purposes at (apparently) the same time. Although the computer actually services each user in sequence, the high speed of the computer makes it appear that the users are all handled simultaneously.

time-slicing The allotment of a portion of processing time to each program in a multiprogramming system to prevent the monopolization of the central processing unit by any one program.

Tiny BASIC A simplified form of the BASIC programming language designed for use on microcomputers. Tiny BASIC is becoming a popular language among microcomputer users. See *BASIC* and *microcomputer*.

T²L Same as TTL.

toggle Pertaining to any device having two stable states. Synonymous with *flip-flop*.

top-down A technique for designing a program or system as major functions and breaking these into even smaller subfunctions. See *modular programming* and *structured programming*.

touch-tone A service mark of the AT & T Co. which identifies its pushbutton dialing service.

tracing routine A routine which provides a time history of the contents of the computer operational registers during the execution of the program. A complete tracing routine would reveal the status of all registers and locations affected by each instruction, each time the instruction is executed.

track A path along which data is recorded on a continuous or rotational medium, such as paper tape, magnetic tape, a magnetic disk or drum.

trailer record A record which follows a group of records and contains pertinent data related to the group of records.

transaction code One or more characters that form part of a record and signify the type of transaction represented by the record.

transaction file Same as *detail file*.

transactions Business or other activities such as, sales, expenditures, shipments, reservations, and inquiries.

transcribe To copy from one external storage medium to another. The process may involve translation.

transducer A device for converting energy from one form to another.

transfer (1) To copy or read, transmit, and store an item or block of information. (2) To change control. See *branch, conditional transfer, jump,* and *unconditional transfer*.

transfer rate The speed at which accessed data can be moved from one device to another. See *access time*.

transformer An alternating current device used in computer power supplies to reduce 115 volts 60 Hertz to a lower more suitable level for conversion to direct current voltage.

transistor A semiconductor device for controlling the flow of current between two terminals, the emitter and the collector, by means of variations in the current flow between a third terminal, the base, and one of the other two. It was developed by Bell Telephone Laboratories.

translator A computer program that performs translations from one language or code to another; e.g., a compiler.

transmit To send data from one location and to receive the data at another location.

trapping A hardware provision for interrupting the normal flow of control of a program while transfer to a known location is made. See *interrupt*.

tree A connected graph with no cycles.

triple precision The retention of three times as many digits of a quantity as the computer normally uses.

troubleshoot A term applied to the task of finding a malfunction in a hardware unit.

TRS-80 A popular, low-cost microcomputer manufactured by Radio Shack.

true complement Synonymous with *ten's complement* and *two's complement*.

truncate To drop digits of a number of terms of a series, thus lessening precision; for example, 3.14159 truncates the series for π, which could conceivably be extended indefinitely.

truncation error An error due to truncation. Contrast with *round-off error*.

TTY An abbreviation for *teletypewriter*.

tunnel diode An electronic device with switching speeds of fractional billionths of seconds. Used in high-speed computer circuitry and memories.

Turing, A.M. (1912-1954) A famous English mathematician and logician who shortly before his death completed the design of one of the world's first modern high-speed digital computers.

turnaround time The time it takes for a job to get from the user to the computing center, to run on the computer and for the program results to be returned back to the user.

turnkey system A computer system selected, designed, programmed, and checked out by another company, a service business, or a computer store, and then turned over to the user. The user has nothing to do but "turn the key" in the front panel lock and start using the system.

twelve-punch A punch in the top row of a Hollerith punched card. Synonymous with *Y-punch*.

two-address computer A computer that employs two addresses in its instruction format. For example, in the instruction ADD A B, the values represented by A and B are added and the result replaces the old value of B.

two-dimensional array An arrangement consisting or rows and columns. See *matrix*.

two's complement A method of representing negative numbers. A positive or negative number is changed to the opposite sign by changing all 1's to 0's and all 0's to 1's, then binarily adding 1. Synonymous with *true complement*.

type font A type face of a given size. See *font*.

typewriter An input/output device which is capable of being connected to a computer and used for communication purposes.

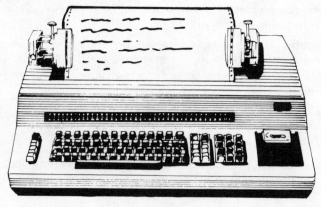

U

μC An abbreviation for microcomputer (**μ** is the Greek letter mu).

ultrafiche Microfiche holding images reduced 100× or more.

ultrasonic Above the human audio range — that is, above 20 kilohertz.

ultraviolet light Used to erase data or instructions stored in an Erasable PROM (EPROM). Once the EPROM has been "erased" it can be reprogrammed by using a PROM programmer. See *EPROM* and *PROM programmer*.

unbundled The position of a computer manufacturer who sells services, programs, training, etc., independently of the computer. Thus, a computer manufacturer who does include his entire line of products and services in a single price is said to be "bundled."

unconditional transfer An instruction that always causes a branch in program control away from the normal sequence of executing instructions. Contrast with *conditional transfer*.

underflow (1) The condition which arises when a computer computation yields a result which is smaller than the smallest possible quantity which the computer is capable of storing. (2) A condition in which the exponent plus the excess becomes negative in a floating point arithmetic operation.

underpunch A punch in either row 1 through row 9 of an 80 column punch card.

union The joining or combining of two or more things.

unipolar Refers to having one pole. See *bipolar*.

unit A device having a special function; e.g., arithmetic unit, central processing unit, or magnetic tape unit.

unit position The extreme right position of a field.

unit record system A data processing system that uses electromechanical processing machines (sorters, collators, etc.) manned by technicians as contrasted with a more automated computerized system. Today, most unit record installations have been replaced with modern computer equipment.

UNIVAC I The first commercial electronic digital computer. It was used by the Census Bureau for processing some of the data from the 1950 census. Forty-eight of these computers were built.

universal language A programming language that is available on many computers; e.g., FORTRAN, COBOL, BASIC. Same as common language.

unpack To separate short units of data that have previously been packed. Opposite of *pack*.

μP An abbreviation for microprocessor. (μ is the Greek letter mu).

update To incorporate into a master file the changes required to reflect transactions or other events.

μs An abbreviation for microsecond; one millionth of a second (μ is the Greek letter mu).

user Anyone who utilizes a computer for problem solving or data manipulation.

user group A group of computer users that share knowledge they have gained and programs they have developed on a computer or class of computers of a specific manufacturer.

user-oriented language See *problem-oriented language* and *procedure-oriented language*.

user terminal See *terminal*.

utility See *computer utility*.

utility routines Software used to perform some frequently required process in the operation of a computer system; e.g., sorting, trigonometric functions, etc. See *systems programs*.

V

vacuum tube The dominant electronic element found in computers prior to the advent of the transistor. Computers using vacuum tubes are referred to as *first generation computers*.

validation The examination of data for correctness against certain criteria, such as format (patterns of numbers, spaces, and letters), ranges (upper and lower value limits), check digits, equivalent entries on a master file.

variable A quantity that can assume any of a given set of values. See *subscripted variable*.

variable-length record Pertaining to a file in which the records are not uniform in length. Contrast with *fixed-length record*.

variable word length Pertaining to a machine word or operand that may consist of a variable number of bits, bytes, or characters. Contrast with *fixed word length*.

VDU An acronym for Visual Display Unit. A peripheral device on which data is displayed on some type of screen.

vector (1) A list or table of numbers, all of which are expressed on the same line. (2) A quantity having magnitude and direction. (3) In computer science, a data structure that permits the location of any item by the use of a single index or subscript. Contrast with a *table, two-dimensional array,* or *matrix,* which requires two subscripts to uniquely locate an item.

vendor A company that sells computers, peripheral devices, time-sharing service or computer services.

Venn diagram A diagram to picture sets and the relationships between sets.

verifier machine A device used to detect keypunching mistakes by rekeying.

verify (1) To determine whether a data processing operation has been accomplished accurately; e.g., to check the results of keypunching. (2) To check data validity.

virtual memory See *virtual storage*.

virtual storage A technique for managing a limited amount of internal storage and a (generally) much larger amount of lower-speed storage in such a way that the distinction is largely transparent to a computer user. The technique entails some means of swapping segments of program and data from the lower-speed storage (which would commonly be a drum or disk) into the internal storage, where it would be interpreted as instructions or operated upon as data. The unit of program or data swapped back and forth is called a *page*. The high-speed storage from which instructions are executed is *real storage*, while the lower-speed storage (drums or disks) is called virtual storage.

visual scanner See *optical character reader.*

voice grade channel A channel which permits transmission of speech.

voice output An audio response output device that permits the computer to deliver answers by the spoken word. Used for stock quotes, credit checks, file inquiry, etc.

volatile storage A storage medium whose contents are lost if power is removed from the system.

von Neumann, John (1903-1957) One of the outstanding mathematicians of this century. He built one of the first electronic computers, contributed much to game theory, and introduced the stored program concept. See *stored program concept.*

wafer A very thin circular slice of cylindrically shaped monocrystalline solid rod of silicon, before or after integrated circuits have been fabricated on it. The wafer is then cut into square "dice", each of which is an individual integrated circuit.

WATFOR A version of FORTRAN developed at the University of Waterloo in Ontario, Canada. WATFIV is a revision of WATFOR.

WATS An acronym for *Wide Area Telephone Service.* A service that permits an unlimited number of calls from one point to any location in a large area. The United States is divided into six WATS zones.

Watson, Thomas J. The guiding spirit of the IBM Corporation. He was a super salesman and president of IBM until 1952. His motto was THINK, and he has made a lot of people, in particular IBM competitors, think long and hard.

weed To discard currently undesirable or needless items from a file.

weighted code A code where each bit position of the code has a weighted value. In the 8-4-2-1 weighted code system the decimal numeral 529 = 0101 0010 1001.

wheel printer A printer with a printing mechanism that contains the printing characters on metal wheels. A type of *line printer.*

An airline travel agent enters and receives information on flight availability through a computer display terminal. The unit allows each agent to be in continuous direct contact with a computer system which maintains passenger lists, flight schedules, and other information vital to the traveler.

whole number A number without a fractional part; e.g., 63, –47, 88.0.

Wide Area Telephone Service A service provided by telephone companies that permits a customer by use of an access line to make data communications in a specific zone on a dial basis for a flat monthly charge.

wideband channel In data communications, a channel wider in bandwidth than a voice grade channel.

Wiener, Norbert (1894-1964) An American scientist who coined the term cybernetics. The founder of a new branch of science, he believed that many thought processes in the human brain could be determined mathematically and adapted for computers. Pioneer in the theory of automata.

wire board See *control panel*.

wired program computer A computer in which the instructions that specify the operations to be performed are specified by the placement and interconnection of wires. The wires are usually held by a removable control panel, allowing limited flexibility of operation. The term is also applied to permanently wired machines which are then called fixed program computers.

word A group of bits, characters, or bytes considered as an entity and capable of being stored in one storage location.

word length The number of bits, characters, or bytes in a word.

working storage Same as *temporary storage*.

WP An acronym for Word Processing. Involves the use of computerized equipment and systems to facilitate the handling of words and text.

write (1) The process of transferring information from the computer to an output medium. (2) To copy data, usually from internal storage to auxiliary storage devices.

write-inhibit ring Used to prevent data from being written over on magnetic tapes.

X

XOR An acronym for Exclusive OR.

X-punch A punch in the eleventh punching position (row 11) of a Hollerith punched card. Synonymous with *eleven-punch*.

X-Y plotter See *plotter*.

Y

Y-punch A punch in the twelfth position (row 12) of a Hollerith card. Also called a high-punch. Synonymous with *twelve-punch*.

Z

zero A numeral normally denoting lack of magnitude. In many computers there are distinct representations for plus and minus zero.

zero flag A flip-flop that goes to logic 1 if the result of an instruction has the value zero.

zero suppression The suppression (e.g., elimination) of nonsignificant zeros in a numeral, usually before or during a printing operation. For example, the numeral 00004763, with zero suppression, would be printed as 4763.

zone punch A punch in the 0, X or Y row on a Hollerith card.

Zuse, Konrad A German pioneer in the development of computing equipment. In 1941, he completed the Zuse Z-3, a machine with some remarkable advanced features. The speed of this machine was about the same as the Mark I.